W. W. Gardner

Bible Inspiration

Plenary and Verbal

W. W. Gardner

Bible Inspiration
Plenary and Verbal

ISBN/EAN: 9783337171445

Printed in Europe, USA, Canada, Australia, Japan

Cover: Foto ©Lupo / pixelio.de

More available books at **www.hansebooks.com**

BIBLE INSPIRATION;

PLENARY AND VERBAL.

BY

W. W. GARDNER, D. D.,

AUTHOR OF "CHURCH COMMUNION," "MISSILES OF TRUTH," ETC.

PHILADELPHIA:
AMERICAN BAPTIST PUBLICATION SOCIETY,
1420 Chestnut Street.

Entered according to Act of Congress, in the year 1886, by the
AMERICAN BAPTIST PUBLICATION SOCIETY,
In the Office of the Librarian of Congress, at Washington.

PREFATORY NOTE.

The following Essay on BIBLE INSPIRATION was read before the BETHEL BAPTIST MINISTER AND DEACON'S MEETING of Southern Kentucky, in 1873, and after free criticism, unanimously requested for publication in permanent form. It was also repeated by invitation before the MINISTER'S MEETING OF THE GENERAL ASSOCIATION OF EAST TENNESSEE, in October, 1874, and after much criticism, unanimously endorsed by that body. When it was requested for publication, the author was performing the double labor of a pastor, and Professor of Theology, in Bethel College, Russellville, Kentucky, and could not command the time to prepare it for the press. Hence it was laid aside until the spring of 1884, when it was expanded into its present form. Free use was made of the works of Carson, Gaussen, Lee, Westcott, and other writers on Inspiration, and due credit given. It claims to have a character of its own, and is believed to present the true theory of Bible Inspiration in a popular form. The times demand something on this vital subject, and it is hoped that this short treatise may, by the divine blessing, be useful to young preachers especially, and to Bible readers generally.

W. W. GARDNER.

BARDSTOWN, KENTUCKY, *July* 4, 1884.

BIBLE INSPIRATION:
PLENARY AND VERBAL.

The Inspiration of the Scriptures is a subject of transcendent importance. It is a fundamental article of that faith which was once delivered to the saints, for which we are required to contend earnestly. With this cardinal doctrine, our holy religion must stand or fall. It settles the question whether or not the Bible is the word of God. Suffer me, then, to invite your serious attention to the *Nature* and *Proofs* of Inspiration, and to the most plausible *Objections* to the doctrine. And as the subject is vast, I can give but an outline of it in this essay.

THE NATURE OF BIBLE INSPIRATION.

What is it?

I. *Inspiration is distinct from Revelation.*

They differ in their very nature. Revelation is a direct communication from God of such knowledge as man either could not of himself attain, or which he did not in fact possess. We have a striking illustration of this in 2 Kings iv. 27.

Inspiration, on the other hand, consists in that actuating, controlling, and guiding influence of the Holy Spirit, under which God's chosen messengers *spoke* and *wrote* the original Scriptures. In short, it denotes that extraordinary divine influence, under the direction and control of which all parts of the original Scriptures were recorded, whether they be direct revelations or mere historical facts. So that the *entire Bible and every part of it* was written by Inspiration, and therefore is true.

Now, Inspiration pertains, not so much to the writers, as to their *writings*. Accordingly, says Paul: "All Scripture is given by inspiration of God, and is profitable," etc. 2 Tim. iii. 16. The meaning of this passage is the same, whether it be rendered, "All Scripture is inspired by God" (Revised Version), or, "All Scripture is given by inspiration of God." In both, the apostle equally attests the fact that *all Scripture is divinely inspired*. Inspiration, therefore, is to be viewed rather in the Book, than in the men; the Book was inspired for all time, the men merely for the time being. Most of the errors on this subject have arisen from viewing inspiration in the writers, rather than in their writings.

In the language of the late Dr. Carson: "The great mistake on this subject has arisen from considering inspiration as it respects the inspired persons; whereas the inspiration in 2 Tim. iii. 16, respects the *things written.* Now, if every part of a writing is given by inspiration, no part of it can be uninspired, or differently inspired. In the relation of the most ordinary fact, God must have given every word of the account, else it cannot be said to be given by his inspiration. Every part of it is the word of God, and the inspiration that records the deepest mysteries cannot go beyond this. Inspiration, as it respects the inspired persons, might have many degrees. But the question is not whether one man may not have been more inspired than another; it is whether one part of Scripture is more inspired than another. The question is independent even of the truth or falsehood of the thing recorded by inspiration. The inspiration of the account of Satan's lies in deceiving our first parents, is as great as that which records the promise, 'The seed of the woman shall bruise the head of the serpent.' . . . It is not said that the sacred writers were inspired with knowledge which they previously possessed. But it is said that their *accounts* of everything recorded by them are given by inspiration; and this is as true with respect to things previously known by them, as it is with respect to things communicated by revelation." "Carson on Inspiration," pp. 229, 230.

Hence it is evident that Inspiration and Revelation are distinct in their very nature. So distinct are they, that the one may exist without the other. For instance, the Patriarchs received *revelations*, but were not inspired to record them. On the other hand, Mark and Luke were *inspired* to record their Gospels; but we are not informed that they ever received a revelation. Indeed, this distinction is radical; for while it is true that Scripture in all its parts is *inspired,* it is not true that all its contents are *revelations;* for it consists partly of historical incidents before known to the writers. Yet the *record* of all is equally inspired, and hence equally true. The narrative portions of the Bible, therefore, whether contained in the historical books of the Old Testament, or in the Gospels and Acts of the Apostles, are to be looked upon as stamped with the same infallible truth as the account of supernatural revelations. Indeed, historical facts formed the *basis* of the New Testament record; and, under divine influence, each writer presented those facts in his own independent narrative. Direct revelations formed the basis of the prophetical books; but such revelations, when once received, correspond to historical narratives, and become the groundwork of the prophetic record, under the guidance of the Holy Spirit.

Moreover, the gift of Inspiration was required equally by those who had received revelations, as by those who had not received them. In the former case, Inspiration was necessary, not only to enable the sacred writer to apprehend and express the divine communications correctly, but also to enable him to record them faithfully and truly long after they had been received. When once a revelation had been received and publicly announced, it then became as much a matter of history as any natural event recorded in the Bible. Now we know that many things contained in the Scriptures were not committed to writing for years after they occurred, as for example, the Mosaic account of creation. In all such cases, Inspiration was indispensable, in order both to bring the original revelation before the mind of the writer in its purity, and to enable him to record it with infallible accuracy. The same was equally true of mere historical events. Hence Jesus promised his apostles and evangelists that the Holy Spirit should bring all things to their *remembrance*, whatsoever he had taught them, as well as show them things to come.

But while Inspiration and Revelation are thus distinct in their nature, still a fixed and necessary relation subsists between them. Revelation without Inspiration would be comparatively useless as an authoritative rule of faith and practice; for without the latter there would be no certainty that the former had been handed down to us correctly. But once establish the truth of Inspiration, and the question is settled forever that we have the pure word of God in the original Scriptures, though we might not be able to trace the history of its transmission with unerring certainty. In short, Inspiration insures and preserves the *integrity of the sacred record*, and banishes every doubt as to the truth of the Bible.

Again, Inspiration and Revelation differ in their *sources*, as well as in their nature. Now God has revealed himself by *act* and by *word*—by act in creation, and by word in the Scriptures; and in both Jesus Christ was the efficient Agent. (See John i. 1-3; Col. i. 16.) In the divine economy, the *Second Person* in the Godhead is the source of all Revelation, while the *Third Person* is the source of all Inspiration. In all ages and under all dispensations, the Eternal Word has been the *Revealer*, and the Eternal Spirit the *Inspirer* of all Scripture truth. These two great facts constitute the pillars upon which must rest the true theory respecting the divine origin and inspiration of the Holy Scriptures. Accordingly, the sacred writers clearly mark this distinction. They invariably ascribe Revelation to Jesus Christ, and Inspiration to the Holy Spirit.

For instance, Peter, in referring to the source of Inspiration, says: "Prophecy came not in old time by the will of man, but holy men of God spake *as they were moved by the Holy Ghost.*" 2 Peter i. 21. And John, in speaking of the source of Revelation, denominates the Scriptures —"*the Revelation of Jesus Christ.*" Rev. i. 1. Both the Moral and the Ceremonial laws, as well as the gospel, were given by Jesus Christ. (Comp. Ps. lxviii. 18 with Eph. iv. 8.) He engraved the Decalogue upon the tables of stone with his own hand, and gave the ceremonial law through angels; and then guided Israel through the wilderness by his presence. (See Acts vii. 30-34, 37, 38; comp. 1 Cor. x. 4-9.)

Revelation is an all-comprehending system, whose *centre* is Christ, from whom all divine comumnications to man have proceeded. He is not only the centre, but the *source* of all Revelation, and not merely the channel through which it flowed. He was "God *manifested* in the flesh"—"the Way, and *the Truth*, and the Life." 1 Tim. iii. 16; John xiv. 6. In the New Testament this fact is most obvious. Here we see the Incarnate Word himself, no longer under the mysterious character of "*The Angel of Jehovah*" (Gen. xvi. 9-11; xxii. 11, 12; Ex. iii. 7), but in his own proper person, fully revealing the divine will which had been partially disclosed through "all his holy prophets since the world began." Acts iii. 21. He did not, indeed, complete the canon of Revelation while on earth. When about to ascend up where he was before, Jesus said to his chosen disciples: "I have yet many things to say unto you, but ye cannot bear them now. Howbeit, when the Spirit of truth is come, he will guide you into all truth: for he shall not speak of himself; but whatsoever he shall hear, that shall he speak: and he will show you things to come. He shall glorify ME; for *he shall receive of mine*, and shall show it unto you." John xvi. 12-14.

Hence we see that the entire system of revealed truth proceeded from Jesus Christ, as the author and source of all Revelation; while the sacred writers were guided and preserved from errors in recording them by the inspiration of the Holy Spirit, who brought all things to their remembrance and showed them things to come. Accordingly, our Lord said: "No man knoweth who the Son is, but the Father; and who the Father is, but the Son, and he to whom the Son will reveal him." Luke x. 22. And Paul, in referring to the source of his knowledge of divine truth, says: "I neither received it of man, neither was I taught it, but *by the revelation of Jesus Christ*" (Gal. i. 12); while he also specifies the agency by which he and his inspired colleagues received revelations—"God hath revealed them unto us *by his Spirit.*" 1 Cor. ii. 10.

Hence it is evident that Revelation and Inspiration differ essentially in their *sources*—the one being the peculiar function of Jesus Christ, and the other being the peculiar function of the Holy Spirit; and this difference is *specific*, and not one of degree, as some suppose.

Now this distinction between Inspiration and Revelation is one of great practical importance, and satisfactorily accounts for the fact, that while some portions of Scripture are pure revelations, and other portions mere historical incidents, still the whole *Scripture record is divinely inspired*, and hence all equally true and equally "*the word of God.*" While Paul declares, therefore, that "*All Scripture is given by inspiration of God, and is profitable,*" John opens his First Epistle by saying: "That which was from the beginning,—*that which we have seen and heard, declare we unto you.*" Thus Inspiration establishes the absolute truthfulness of all parts of the Scripture record, whether they be matters of direct revelation, or mere historical facts; for it should be ever borne in mind that Inspiration extends alike to all parts of Scripture, and stamps the whole Bible as *the word of God* in the highest sense of the term. Inspiration does not vouch for the truth or falsity of what is recorded, for it records Satan's lies; but it does vouch for the *correctness of the record itself*, and insures its truthfulness, as a faithful record.

Hence we see that Inspiration is essentially distinct from Revelation, both as to its *nature* and *source*, though they are intimately related to each other in the Scriptures.

II. *Inspiration is distinct from the ordinary influences of the Holy Spirit.*

They differ in several important respects. The ordinary influences of the Holy Spirit have been enjoyed by believers in all ages; Inspiration was enjoyed only by God's chosen messengers. The one is *ordinary* and *permanent:* the other was *extraordinary* and *temporary,* like the gift of miracles. The former, though constant, varies in degree according to our faith and faithfulness; the latter was only *occasional,* and did not admit of degrees. None but the truly pious enjoy the ordinary influences of the Holy Spirit; but Inspiration, like the gift of prophecy, was in no sense dependent on the personal holiness of those who received it. Nor was Inspiration subject to the will of the sacred writers. Like Prophecy, it "came not by the will of man." Indeed, it often led them contrary to their own wills. For example, Paul, at one time, purposed to preach the gospel in Asia, but "was forbidden of the Holy Ghost"; and he "attempted to go into Bithynia, but the Spirit suffered him not" (Acts xvi. 6–10) at that time. Inspiration was enjoyed and exercised according to the sovereign will of God.

The sacred writers, in common with all believers, enjoyed the ordinary influences of the Holy Spirit at all times, but they were inspired only at *intervals*—only when *officially declaring and recording the word of God*. On all other occasions they enjoyed the same kind of spiritual influence that other Christians enjoyed, and were as fallible as other ministers of equal piety—"men of like passions as ourselves." Acts xiv. 15. They carried their treasure "in earthen vessels." 2 Cor. iv. 7. Hence Peter, on one occasion, *denied* his Lord with oaths (Matt. xxvi. 69–75), and, on another occasion, *dissembled* at Antioch and was blamable (Gal. ii. 11–13.); while Barnabas and Paul had a *sharp contention* about John Mark, and thenceforth separated in their labors. Acts xv. 36–41. But when acting under the influence of Inspiration, there was neither imperfection in their conduct nor fallibility in their teaching or writing. The Holy Spirit exercised an absolute control over their acts and words and pens on such occasions. Hence the absence of personal feeling and the suppression of personal emotion throughout the Scripture narrative; every tendency which is merely human being neutralized and suppressed. But it was only when acting in their official capacity as inspired teachers and writers, that our blessed Lord promised them the unerring guidance of his Holy Spirit. Nor do they ever claim infallibility in any other capacity. The Inspiration of the sacred writers, therefore, was wholly objective, and designed to furnish mankind with a pure Bible; while the ordinary influences of the Holy Spirit are altogether subjective, and designed to promote the comfort and sanctification of individual Christians.

This distinction is radical; and it at once shows the absurdity of the theory of degrees in Inspiration, advocated by Bishop Wilson, Dr. John Dick, and others. Doubtless the sacred writers, in common with their fellow Christians, enjoyed divine direction, elevation, and superintendence, but these do not constitute Inspiration. The gift of Inspiration was extraordinary, and hence as distinct from the ordinary influences of the Holy Spirit as was the gift of miracles. Now there are degrees in these ordinary influences of the Spirit, but there are no degrees in Inspiration. "*All Scripture* is given by inspiration of God and is profitable," because all is equally inspired, and hence equally true. Paul's directions to Timothy respecting his cloak left at Troas, though less important, contain as much inspiration as his profoundest doctrines. Even the sayings of wicked men and of devils are recorded by inspiration, as truly as the sayings of Christ himself. There is nothing in Scripture, however unimportant in itself, that is not inspired, and inspired in precisely the same sense as the most important. Hence we see that Inspiration is distinct from the ordinary influences of the Holy Spirit, and ceased when its great object was accomplished, while the gracious influences of the Spirit will continue to the end of time.

III. *Inspiration combines divine agency with human instrumentality in one harmonious whole.*

This is an unquestionable fact, however it may be explained. On the one hand, God has given us a revelation of his character and will; on the other hand, he has expressed it in human language and recorded it by men. Hence the Bible has both a divine and human aspect, while it is all the word of God.

Yet this fact has given rise to two opposite theories of Inspiration equally remote from the truth. One theory virtually excludes divine agency by giving undue prominence to human instrumentality; the other practically ignores human instrumentality by dwelling too exclusively upon divine agency. But neither of these theories satisfies the conditions of revelation, or accounts for the obvious facts of Scripture. Hence some have been led to deny all Inspiration, while others have virtually explained it away.

But the truth on this subject is found midway between these extremes. According to the true theory of Inspiration, divine agency and human instrumentality are inseparably blended together in one harmonious whole in revelation; and what God hath joined together, let not man separate. In whatever light we view the Scriptures, we are bound to recognize the combination of divine influence with human utterance; and both are necessary to a revelation from God to man. Without divine agency, the Bible could not be the word of God; without human instrumentality, it would not be intelligible to man. As in nature, so in revelation, God accomplishes his ends by the use of appropriate means. Here, the end is the communication of divine truth to man; while the means consist in exhibiting that truth in accordance with man's nature. That man may be able to grasp the truth, it must be allied to human conceptions, and clothed in human language. Thought is wedded to language as necessarily as the soul is to the body. Indeed, language is a condition of our being, fixing the conception as well as the communication of thought. Without language the visions of the prophet would have been confused shadows, but with it they became instructive lessons. It was not enough that divine truth should be revealed to the inspired teacher, he must be able to express it in intelligible language. And when thus expressed, human agency became an integral part of the divine message.

Now, in order to accomplish this object, the Author of revelation selected his own agents; and the ground of his choice was clearly their natural and acquired fitness for the work. In the providence of God, Moses was skilled in all the wisdom of the Egyptians; and Paul was thoroughly instructed, first in in the university at Tarsus, and then in the theological school at Jerusalem, so that he could address both Jews and Gentiles in the words of their own learned writers. Westcott's Introduction, pp. 30-40.

Even the traits of individual character and peculiarities of thought and style displayed in the composition of Scripture, were essential to the perfect exhibition of the truth. The Holy Spirit did not employ the sacred writers as lifeless machines, but as rational agents, whose genius, natural temperament, and personal characteristics were blended and combined with his all-controlling and guiding influence. Indeed, it was only by calling into active exercise the personal peculiarities of the several writers that divine truth could be adapted to human comprehension and brought home to the hearts of mankind. Thus the harmonious combination of divine influence with human agency in revelation, preserves absolute truthfulness with perfect adaptation and intelligibility; and renders the language as perfect as the thought. And thus revelation reflects the image of its Incarnated Author, in whom the divine and human exist in the highest form and in the most perfect union.

It is a leading feature of this theory of Inspiration, that the Holy Spirit employed man's faculties in accordance with their natural laws, and operated *by*, and *through*, and *with* the sacred writers as active, conscious agents. He acted as an infinitely rational Agent on finitely rational subjects, in accordance with the laws of mind. Thus, humanity, instead of being paralyzed and suppressed, became an integral part of the agency employed; and hence the peculiar type of each writer's mind is enstamped upon his writings. Divine influence embraced the entire activity and resources of the human agents, using their faculties, knowledge, and style at pleasure, and rendering their very language the word of God. Each writer, under the actuating and controlling influence of the Holy Spirit, made use of all the information in his possession, whether supplied by natural means or by direct revelation. This fact, as we have seen, forms the basis of the distinction between Inspiration and Revelation. Many things recorded in the

Scriptures are not matters of Revelation; but this in no sense invalidates the truth that the entire record is inspired, and that everything in the Bible is the word of God, and has been transmitted to us under the influence of Inspiration. The Holy Spirit provided that each and every portion of Scripture should convey such information as best subserved the divine purpose and human good, irrespective of the character of that information—whether it consisted of known historical facts, or pure revelations from God.

Nor are we to suppose that Inspiration extended merely to the doctrines and facts recorded by the sacred writers. We find the same divine guidance and control claimed for the language which they employed. "Which things we speak," says Paul, "not *in the words* which man's wisdom teacheth, but *which the Holy Ghost teacheth.*" 1 Cor. ii. 13. Thus we see that divine influence and human agency were not simply concurrent, but *absolutely amalgamated and combined into one distinct energy in revelation*, so that Paul could say to the Thessalonians: "When ye received the word of God which ye heard of us, ye received it not as the word of men, but as it is in truth, *the word of God.*" 1 Thess. ii. 13.

The harmonious blending of the divine and human intelligence in the composition of Scripture, is distinctly recognized by Christ and his apostles. They frequently quote from the Old Testament and attribute the words interchangeably to God and to the sacred writers. For instance, Matthew represents Jesus as quoting the Fourth Commandment thus: "God commanded, saying, Honor thy father and thy mother" (Matt. xv. 4); while Mark records the parallel passage as follows: "For *Moses* said, Honor thy father and thy mother." Mark vii. 10. And Paul applied the language of prophecy to the Jews at Rome thus: "Well spake the Holy Ghost by Esaias the prophet," etc. (Acts xxviii. 25), while John quotes the same passage as follows: "These things said *Esaias,*" etc. John xii. 41. Hence the Evangelist could say of prophecy in general: "All this was done, that it might be fulfilled which was spoken of *the Lord by the prophet.*" Matt. i. 22. No artificial line of distinction, therefore, can be drawn between divine agency and human instrumentality in revelation, any more than between light and heat in the sun. They are so combined as to constitute one and the same energy.

In the New Testament, this harmonious blending of the divine and human intelligence is expressly declared. For instance, Jesus said to his apostles: "Ye are *witnesses* of these things; and behold, I send the promise of my Father upon you." Luke xxiv. 48, 49. And Peter declares the fulfillment of this promise: "*We* are his witnesses of these things, and so is also the Holy Ghost." Acts v. 32. Thus we have the joint testimony of the

Holy Spirit and of the sacred writers to the fulfillment of another promise of the Saviour: "The Comforter, whom I will send unto you from the Father, shall testify of me, and ye also shall bear witness" (John xv. 26, 27); a pledge to which Peter evidently alludes when he declares of himself and his inspired colleagues, that they "preached the gospel with the Holy Ghost sent down from heaven." 1 Peter i. 12. All such passages clearly teach, that the Holy Spirit and the apostles conjointly bore testimony to the truth of the gospel, and co-operated in the formation of the New Testament Scriptures; in other words, that the Holy Spirit operated *by* and *through* and *with* the agency of Christ's chosen witnesses, in perfect harmony with the laws of their nature. Moreover, such expressions illustrate the fact that God, even in bestowing the gift of Inspiration, made use of those *natural* means whereby the *inspired* testimony of his servants should have the utmost credibility which *uninspired* human testimony could claim. Hence it is that the preaching of the apostles is invariably represented in the New Testament as *infallible testimony*, and that peculiar importance is attached to the fact of their having been *eye-witnesses* of the events of Christ's life. In proof of this, see Acts ii. 32; iii. 15; x. 39; 1 John i. 1–3; 2 Peter i. 16–18; Rev. i. 2. Hence Paul appeals to the fact that he had *seen* Jesus Christ as proof of his apostleship. 1 Cor. ix. 1. Now, if we combine with this the statement of James, by which he prefaced the decision of the council at Jerusalem, "It seemed good to *the Holy Ghost and to us*" (Acts xv. 28),—the conclusion is strengthened, that there was a perfectly harmonious blending of the divine and the human intelligences in the composition of the Holy Scriptures. Thus the human testimony of the sacred writers was exalted into divine testimony by the co-operation and Inspiration of the Spirit of God, in perfect accordance with the laws of mind.

The co-existence of divine agency and human instrumentality in revelation accounts for the fact, that on every page of Scripture we perceive evident traces of the individuality and personal characteristics of the different writers. Even when acting as the official organs of the Holy Spirit, the sacred writers exhibit styles quite dissimilar—they pursue different trains of thought, view the same truth from different points of view, and present it in different lights: such individual peculiarities being, in fact, the means which God has wisely employed to give a human coloring to his truth, and to adapt it to the various capacities and wants of mankind. Thus divine truth, in a sense, became incarnate. Hence the logical mind of Paul; the practical temperament of James; the chastened boldness of Peter; and the affectionate and loving heart of John,—are all distinct in their respective writings, and were actively employed in conveying that portion of the divine message best suited to each; while the Holy Spirit inspired and linked together the various parts of Scripture, so as to form one harmonious and vitally organized whole; each part serving its appropriate purpose, and each conveying its own portion of the truth as it is in Jesus. While, then, the Scriptures are the writings of Moses and the Prophets, the Evangelists and the Apostles, they are *the word of God in language, matter, and style;* for all was given by inspiration of God. The entire form and substance of Scripture, therefore, whether resulting from natural knowledge or divine revelation, have been assimilated and combined into one homogeneous organism by the vital energy of the Holy Spirit.

Now, God has not only revealed his will to man *gradually*—"by little and by little"—but he has also made use of certain events from time to time, which formed a kind of *natural channel* for the conveyance of his truth. As in prophecy generally, each prediction was called forth by and attached itself to certain events occurring at the time of its utterance; so the external occasions which called forth the successive portions of the New Testament may be regarded as the providential element by which the full agency of the sacred writers was brought under the influence of Inspiration. Each writer acted voluntarily, and wrote with an earnest purpose to meet the then existing wants of the churches and individuals whom he addressed. For example, the Epistles of Paul to the Corinthians were called forth by certain events in one of the churches which he had planted, and the apostle wrote for the special instruction of that church. Yet such was the occasion made use of by the Holy Spirit for the purpose of conveying divine instruction to all succeeding churches in similar circumstances. Thus "*all Scripture*" given by inspiration of God, "is *profitable* for doctrine, for reproof, for correction, for instruction in righteousness," and is equally adapted to all ages and climes.

Hence the Bible, like its Incarnate Author, bears the impress both of divinity and humanity in harmonious and inseparable union, and is perfectly adapted to the condition and wants of man. Divine truth was cast in human moulds, and hence has a human form. And thus it is that human instrumentality has been moulded by divine influence into the very organism of Scripture. Every ray of Divine Light has been borne to mankind through the medium best suited to its transmission ; and yet, while borrowing its particular hue from the medium through which it passed, it retains all the purity of the Sun of righteousness from which it emanated.

Such, then, is the nature of Inspiration, or what it is. *It is distinct from Revelation ; and distinct from the ordinary influences of the Holy Spirit; while it combines divine agency with human instrumentality in one har-*

monious whole. This theory of Inspiration satisfies all the conditions of revelation, and accounts for the peculiar phenomena of Scripture. 1. The distinction between Inspiration and Revelation satisfactorily accounts for the fact that "*all Scripture*" is divinely inspired and equally inspired, whether it consist of direct revelations from God or of mere historical facts previously known to the sacred writers; and that the *entire record*, and *every word of it*, was given by divine inspiration, and hence is infallibly true. 2. The distinction between Inspiration and the ordinary influences of the Holy Spirit accounts for the additional fact, that, while the divine writers were fallible and liable to err when acting merely in their individual capacity as Christians, they were absolutely infallible and incapable of erring when acting in their official capacity as inspired teachers; and hence they claim divine authority and perfect truthfulness for all their teachings and writings. 3. That the harmonious combination of divine agency and human instrumentality in the communication and composition of the Scriptures fully explains the fact that the Bible possesses both a divine and human aspect, inseparably combined together, and that the individuality and personal peculiarities of the different writers appear on every page of their writings; while the Holy Spirit employed all the faculties and resources of the several writers, rendering even their language the word of God. Hence the absurdity of the theory, that the subject-matter only of Scripture is inspired, while its language was left to the unaided choice of the writers. On the contrary, the whole of Scripture, language, manner, and matter, is divinely inspired, and hence all is the word of God.

DIRECT PROOFS OF INSPIRATION.

Having briefly explained the Nature of Inspiration, let us consider—

II. *The Direct Proofs of Inspiration.*

The evidences of the truth of the Bible are of two kinds, *external* and *internal.* The external evidences embrace *Miracles,* *Prophecy,* the *Success* of the gospel, etc.; and the internal evidences include the *superhuman revelations* of the Bible, *its heavenly spirit,* its *moral rectitude,* its *peculiar doctrines,* its wonderful *harmony and unity,* its *perfect adaptation,* and *its beneficial effects* on individuals and nations. These evidences are clear and conclusive, and fully satisfy every honest inquirer after the truth. No other book has a tithe of the evidence of its truth, and hence the Bible is its own witness. But we cannot here present these evidences; and in the present essay, we must take for granted the entire array of Christian evidence—embracing both the external and internal evidences of Christianity, together with the vast extent of antiquarian and grammatical criticism, and the profound argument from the analogy of nature, as well as the concurrent belief of the wise and good of all ages, and the harmonious testimony of sacred and profane history. On such evidence, we are fully authorized to assume the authenticity, genuineness, and absolute truthfulness of Scripture, and to draw our main arguments for the Inspiration of the Bible from its own pages.

Nor is this view of the subject justly chargeable with logical fallacy. "As well might we reject the personal statements of an ambassador, with respect to the nature of his powers and the source of his instructions, after we had verified his credentials, and satisfied ourselves as to his veracity. And thus the adducing of arguments from Scripture itself, in proof of its own inspiration, is no *petitio principii*. It would only become so, were we to assume the fact of its inspiration in order to infer therefrom the *credibility* of its contents. This credibility we establish by independent proofs. Still less can any objection be made to our drawing inferences as to the nature of the influence under which the Bible was composed, from the phenomena which its pages present to view, or its contents record. Such a process of reasoning is as sound as it is philosophical."—Wm. Lee, on "Inspiration of Scripture," p. 98.

And the evidence furnished by the inspired writers themselves is necessarily of the highest value; for they alone could bear direct testimony to the fact, that they had received revelations from God, and were divinely authorized and inspired to record them. All other evidence is merely circumstantial and inferential. Their testimony, therefore, is legitimate and must be received as direct proof of Inspiration, and as the strongest proof that can be given on the subject.

Now the truth of the Bible being established by its own proper evidences, its Inspiration becomes as much a matter of revelation as is justification by faith, or salvation by grace. Both stand equally on the authority of Scripture; and all who admit the truth of the Bible are bound to admit its obvious teachings on this subject. There is, in fact, no other way of establishing Inspiration but by revelation; and this question must be settled by the Scriptures themselves just as any other question of revealed truth. Then, "to the law and to the testimony; if they speak not according to this word, it is because there is no light in them." Isa. viii. 20. But we can give only a specimen of direct Scripture proof, at present, omitting all collateral proofs.

1. My first direct proof of Inspiration is drawn *from the Writings of Moses and the Prophets.*

Moses was indeed a prophet, but he was more than a prophet. He was the mediator of the old covenant (Gal. iii. 19); and a lively type of Jesus Christ, the Mediator of the new covenant. Heb. xii. 24. When called to his high office on Mount Horeb, he humbly plead to be excused, saying: "Alas, O my Lord, I am not eloquent;"—adding, "send, I pray thee, by the hand of him whom thou wilt send." The Lord answered: "Who hath made man's mouth? Now therefore go, and I will be with thy mouth, and will teach thee what thou shalt say." Ex. iv. 10-13. Moses obeyed, and became mighty in words and in deeds.

Now the Old Testament was divided by the Jews into three parts: the Law of Moses, the Prophets, and the Psalms; and this division was recognized by our Saviour. Luke xxiv. 44. The first part embraces the Pentateuch, or five Books of Moses, and consists of direct revelations, prophetical and typical predictions, and numerous historical facts. In the composition of these sacred books divine Inspiration was indispensable, both as to the facts and language; for Moses wrote them long after creation, an account of which he was commissioned to give. Accordingly, Moses claimed to speak and write by divine authority and under the inspiration of the Holy Spirit; and his claim was supported by wonderful miracles, as well as by the superhuman character of his writings, and the immemorial beliefs of God's people. He claimed that his commands were the commands of God; that his teachings were divine teachings; and that his writings were the inspired word of God.

Hence Moses, in recapitulating his teachings, just before his death, said to Israel: "Ye shall not add unto the word which I command you, neither shall ye diminish aught from it, that ye may keep *the commandments of the Lord your God which I commanded you.*" Deut. iv. 2. And in summing up all his teachings, he added: "Now these are the commandments, the statutes, and the judgments which the Lord your God commanded to teach you, that ye might do them." Deut. vi. 1. And Moses was expressly and repeatedly commanded to commit to *writing* the several portions of the Pentateuch, embracing even the travels and sins of the children of Israel. For instance, "The Lord said unto Moses, *Write this for a memorial in a book,* and rehearse it in the ears of Joshua; for I will utterly put out the remembrance of Amalek from under heaven." Ex. xvii. 14. Again, "The Lord said unto Moses, *Write thou these words;* for after the tenor of these words I have made a covenant with thee and with Israel." Ex. xxxiv. 27. And again, it is said: "These are the journeys of the children of Israel, which went forth out of the land of Egypt with their armies under the hand of Moses and Aaron. And Moses wrote their goings out according to their journeys, *by the commandment of the Lord.*" Num. xxxiii. 1, 2. "And it came to pass, *when Moses had made an end of writing the words of this law in a book, until they were finished,* that Moses commanded the Levites, who bare the ark of the covenant of the Lord, saying: Take this book of the law, and put it in the side of the ark of the covenant." Deut. xxxi. 24–26. Accordingly, Paul, in alluding to the facts of Jewish history, says: "All these things happened unto them for our example; and *they are written for our admonition.*" 1 Cor. x. 11. Hence we see that the Law of Moses, embracing the first five books of the Old Testament, was written by divine Inspiration, and is a part of the word of God.

The same is equally true of the writings of Samuel, Isaiah, Jeremiah, and all the prophets, including the second division of the Old Testament Scriptures. God expressly promised Inspiration to his ancient servants. For example, when Jeremiah plead that he could not speak on account of his youth, the Lord answered: "Say not, I am a child; for thou shalt go to all that I shall send thee, and whatsoever I command thee thou shalt speak;" and having reached forth his hand and touched his young servant's mouth, he said: "*Behold, I have put my words in thy mouth.*" Jer. i. 5–9. So the Lord said to Isaiah, Ezekiel, and all his servants. They were commissioned and inspired to speak and write *his* words, whether men would hear or forbear. See Ezek. iii. 10–12.

Accordingly, all the prophets claimed to speak and write by divine Inspiration. Hence the frequency of the expressions with which they introduce their messages: "Hear the word of the Lord" (Isa. i. 10); "For the mouth of the Lord hath spoken it" (Isa. i. 20); "Thus saith the Lord" (Jer. xvi. 9); "The word of the Lord that came to Jeremiah the prophet" (Jer. xlvii. 1); "The word of the Lord came expressly unto Ezekiel the priest" (Ezek. i. 3); "The word of the Lord came unto Jonah the second time" (Jonah iii. 1). The divine message came to the prophets only when God pleased, and often in an unexpected way. As it is written: "It came to pass the same night, that the word of God came to Nathan, saying" (1 Chron. xvii. 3); "The hand of the Lord was upon me, and carried me out in the Spirit of the Lord" (Ezek. xxxvii. 1); "The word of God came unto John in the wilderness" (Luke iii. 2). Thus God spake at pleasure by and through *his* servants as rational agents; and hence their words were *his* words.

Indeed, divine Inspiration was indispensable to the prophetic office; for the prophets themselves often could not understand the meaning of their own predictions. Daniel, for example, tells us more than once, that he did not understand the prophetic meaning of his own words. Says he: "I heard, but I understood not: then said I, O my Lord, what shall be the end of these things? And he said, Go thy way, Daniel: for the words are closed up and sealed till the time of the end." Dan. xii. 8, 9. And Peter informs us that "the prophets inquired and searched diligently" to understand the full meaning of their own predictions, "searching what, or what manner of time *the Spirit of Christ* which was in them did signify, when it testified beforehand the sufferings of Christ, and the glory that should follow." 1 Peter i. 10, 11.

Now all prophecy is necessarily obscure as to details until its fulfillment. In the language of Irenæus, "every prophecy is an enigma before its accomplishment." This necessity arises from two causes: First, from the nature of the case, the full meaning of prophetic language must transcend our limited comprehension; and, Second, without such obscurity, the full course of history would be interrupted. The obscurity of prophecy was evidently designed to leave the freedom of human actions undisturbed. It is on this principle that Paul states that, had the rulers of this world understood the mystery of redemption as revealed in prophecy, they would not have crucified the Lord of glory. 1 Cor. ii. 8. See also Acts xiii. 27. That the predictions of Scripture were not designed to be fully understood before their fulfillment, is clearly indicated by our Lord when he says: "And now I have told you before it come to pass, that *when it is come to pass* ye might believe." John xiv. 29. Thus it is that unfulfilled prophecy is compared by Peter to "a light that shineth in a dark place, until the day dawn, and the day-star arise in your hearts" by its fulfillment. 2 Peter i. 19. All is plain when the event occurs.

BIBLE INSPIRATION. 35

The prophets not only "spake as they were moved by the Holy Ghost" (2 Peter i. 21), but they also *recorded* their predictions by the command of God and under the influence of divine Inspiration. When Samuel had made known to Israel the character of Saul's reign, he "*wrote it in a book*, and laid it up before the Lord." 1 Sam. x. 25. Isaiah was expressly commanded to write his prediction against rebellious Israel on a table, "*and note it in a book*, that it may be for the time to come, forever and ever." Isa. xxx. 8. And we are informed as to the authority and manner in which Jeremiah wrote his predictions: "This word came unto Jeremiah from the Lord, saying: *Take thee a roll of a book, and write therein all the words that I have spoken* against Israel, and against Judah, and against all the nations, from the day I spake unto thee, from the days of Josiah, even unto this day . . . Then Jeremiah called Baruch the son of Neriah: and *Baruch wrote from the mouth of Jeremiah all the words of the Lord, which he had spoken unto him, upon a roll of a book.*" Jer. xxxvi. 1, 2, 4. Similar commands were given to Ezekiel (xxiv. 1, 2; xliii. 10, 11), and to the other prophets. Thus they spake and wrote in obedience to the divine command, " as they were moved by the Holy Ghost."

The prophets not only spake and wrote by divine authority and under divine Inspiration, but they also refer to each other's writings as the infallible word of

God. For example, Daniel quotes by name the predictions of Jeremiah respecting the captivity of Israel. Says he: "I Daniel understood by books the number of the years, whereof the word of the Lord came to Jeremiah the prophet." Dan. ix. 2. And the heavenly messenger who was sent to instruct Daniel, said: "I will show thee that which is noted in the Scripture of truth." Dan. x. 21. Nehemiah tells us how Ezra read and explained "the book of the law of Moses which the Lord had commanded to Israel." Neh. viii. 1. And in his solemn confession of the sins of Israel, he adds: "Many years didst thou forbear them, and testifiedst against them *by thy Spirit in thy prophets.*" Neh. ix. 30. Many similar allusions may be found in the writings of the prophets. Thus the prophets bear separate and united testimony to the divine authority and inspiration of this important part of Old Testament Scripture.

Moreover, God prescribed the ways and means by which his word should be preserved pure from every admixture of error. Those claiming to be prophets were required to furnish, on all proper occasions, the *external proofs* of a divine commission. These proofs consisted of unquestionable Miracles, in addition to the consciousness of a divine call. Now Prophecy, from its embracing the far future, serves as a standing witness to every age, and its testimony strengthens with its fulfillment. But Miracles, by virtue of the evident display of divine power in them, afford to all candid minds the strongest immediate proofs of Inspiration. The language of unprejudiced reason must ever be—"We know that thou art a teacher come from God: for no man can do these miracles that thou doest, except God be with him." John iii. 2. Miracles attest both the messenger and his message, and seal his instructions as divine. Accordingly, John says of the miracles of Christ: "Many other signs truly did Jesus in the presence of his disciples which are not written in this book; but *these are written*, that ye might believe that Jesus is the Christ, the Son of God." John xx. 30, 31. And Paul regards such proofs as indispensable to an apostle, as they were to the ancient prophets. "Truly," says he, "the signs of an apostle were wrought among you in all patience, in signs, and wonders, and mighty deeds." 2 Cor. xii. 12. These external proofs were given at all times when occasion required it; as for example, to Moses, to Gideon, to Hezekiah, and to others. See Ex. iv. 1–9; Judges vi. 36–40; 2 Kings xx. 8–11.

In addition to this, it was expressly enjoined in the Law of Moses, that false prophets should be put to death (Deut. xiii. 1–3; xviii. 20–23); and this injunction was rigidly enforced to the latest period of prophecy. Even parents were required to thrust a son through who was known to prophesy falsely. Zech. xiii.

3. The permanent obligation of these precepts, together with the astonishing care and fidelity with which the Jews guarded the purity of their Scriptures, enables us clearly to discern the *criteria* by which Ezra and Nehemiah were guided in the selection of those books which were known to be inspired; for, aside from their own inspiration, they would have admitted no book as divine which was not recognized as such by the Jews generally. Thus these inspired men were divinely guided to select from the literature of the nation those documents *only* " which had been written for our learning " at the express command of God. Hence the words of the prophets are said to have been "graven on a rock, and written with iron." And had they not have been so engraven and written, by irresistible evidence of their inspiration, how could they have withstood the odium and opposition which they provoked?

From all this it is evident that the Author of Scripture designed that its several parts combined should constitute a perpetual witness for him, and an infallible rule of faith and practice for his people.

But the *Psalms*, as well as the writings of Moses and the Prophets, bear witness to the Inspiration of the Old Testament Scriptures. The several writers of the Psalms are called prophets by our Saviour. Matt. xiii. 35; xxiii. 34. And David, the chief writer, was a prophet (Acts ii. 30); but, like Moses, he was more than a prophet. In his kingly office, he was a striking type of the Messiah, the King of kings. David claimed to speak and write by divine Inspiration. Says he: "*The Spirit of the Lord spake by me, and his word was in my tongue*" (2 Sam. xxiii. 1, 2); and "*this shall be written for the generations to come.*" Ps. cii. 18. Accordingly, Jesus quotes Psalm cx. 1, and says: "David himself said *by the Holy Ghost*, The Lord said to my Lord, Sit thou on my right hand, till I make thine enemies thy footstool." Mark xii. 36. Peter also said: "Men and brethren, this Scripture must needs have been fulfilled, which *the Holy Ghost by the mouth of David spake before* concerning Judas." Acts i. 16. And all the apostles "lifted up their voices to God with one accord, and said: Lord, thou art God—who by the mouth of thy servant David hast said," etc. Acts. iv. 23–25; comp. Ps. ii. 1, 2.

Many other proofs of the Inspiration of the Scriptures might be drawn from the Psalms, but more are unnecessary after what has been given from the writings of Moses and the Prophets. Hence we see that the whole of the Old Testament, and every part of it, was given by Inspiration of God and is profitable.

2. My second direct proof of Inspiration is drawn *from the teachings of the Saviour.*

In previous ages, God had spoken to the fathers "at sundry times and in divers manners" by the prophets. Heb. i. 1. The various parts of revelation were thus conveyed gradually and under aspects best suited to the times; and this progressive development of the divine character and will was rendered necessary by man's incapacity to receive a full revelation at once. But "in these last days God hath spoken unto us by his Son" (verse 2), "who hath abolished death, and hath brought life and immortality to light through the gospel." 2 Tim. i. 10. Thus the light of revelation gradually increased, until the Sun of righteousness himself arose upon our benighted world with healing in his beams. "That was the true Light, which lighteth every man that cometh into the world." John i. 9.

As before shown, Christ is the *centre*, as well as the source of all revelation. Every prophetic announcement and every typical offering and sacrifice pointed to him as "the Lamb of God, which taketh away the sin of the world." John i. 29. There is, therefore, an inseparable connection, as well as perfect harmony, between the Old and the New Testaments. "The law was our schoolmaster to bring us unto Christ" (Gal. iii. 24), "upon whom the ends of the world are come." 1 Cor. x. 11. The object of each successive revelation was to restore the lost truths of religion, and to bring man back to the knowledge and worship of the true God. To attain this great end, different dispensations were necessary, each preparatory to the next, and all preparatory to the present dispensation. The dispensation introduced by Christ, therefore, includes and perfects all previous revelations, and combines them into one harmonious and organized whole complete in all its parts. It perfects both the legal and promissory parts of the Old Testament. The law becomes real, living truth; the promises become actual grace, as it is written: "The law was given by Moses, but grace and truth came by Jesus Christ." John i. 17. Its individuality is now stamped with universality: "Many shall come from the east and west, and shall sit down with Abraham, and Isaac, and Jacob, in the kingdom of heaven." Matt. viii. 11. The middle wall of partition is broken down, and both Jews and Gentiles have become "fellow citizens with the saints and of the household of God." Eph. ii. 18-22.

Accordingly, our Lord throughout his entire ministry, represents himself as fulfilling, *in Person*, the prophetic and typical predictions of the Old Testament Dispensation, and as "blotting out the handwriting of ordinances that was against us." Col. ii. 14. He made the Old Testament the *basis* of his teachings, and continually employed it as the inspired word of God; thus indicating not only its permanent authority, but also its true relation to the New Testament. Hence said he: "Think not that I am come to destroy the law or the prophets: I am not come to destroy, but to fulfill." Matt. v. 17. In these words Christ asserts the inseparable connection between the Old and the New Testaments. He teaches,

First, The divine authority of the Old Testament; second, That the New Testament is the fulfillment of the Old; and third, That, in this sense, the law is not abrogated, but remains an imperishable part of the word of God which we know endureth forever. 1 Peter i. 25. And hence he adds: "Till heaven and earth pass, one jot or one tittle shall in nowise pass from the law, till all be fulfilled." Ver. 18. Jesus here employs the same language to express the permanency of the Old Testament Scriptures, that he elsewhere applies to his own teachings: "Heaven and earth shall pass away, but my words shall not pass away" (Matt. xxiv. 35); that is, the Old Testament Scriptures and the sayings of Christ are alike imperishable, because both are equally the inspired word of God. Hence we must see that the Old Testament was the basis of the New, and received its fulfillment in it. It was the shadow of good things to come, while Christ was the substance. When Messiah came, the positive[1] part of the Old Testament ceased to be binding as a rule of duty, but all the moral part was brought forward and incorporated into the New. Hence both Jews and Gentiles are said to be "built upon the foundation of the apostles and prophets, Jesus Christ himself being the chief corner-stone." Eph. ii. 20. And hence, too, we see

---

[1] This term is used in the same sense as in those cases where positive and moral laws are contrasted—the positive law issued for a special occasion, and of temporary obligation; the moral law such as is everywhere and at all times binding.—ED.

the Christian element in the manna from heaven (John vi. 58); in the narrative of Hagar and Ishmael (Gal. iv. 24–26); in the rock smitten by Moses (1 Cor. x. 4); in the support of the priesthood (1 Cor. ix. 7–14); and in all the Mosaic rites and ceremonies. Heb. ix. 1–24. Thus the New Testament was the key to unlock the Old.

But more particularly we ask: How did Jesus Christ regard the Old Testament Scriptures? What use did he make of them? And what does he say of them? His holy life and heavenly teachings must answer these important questions. Let us then accompany "the Apostle and High Priest of our profession, *Christ Jesus*" (Heb. iii. 1), as he goes forth on his mission of love, bearing "*the volume of the book in which it is written of him.*" Psalm xl. 6–8; comp. Heb. x. 5–10.

Having "fulfilled all righteousness" (Matt. iii. 15), "Jesus was led up of the Spirit into the wilderness, to be tempted of the devil." Matt. iv. 1–11. There, as did the first Adam in Eden, he encountered the Prince of darkness bent on his overthrow. And how did the Son of God repel the subtle attacks of his arch-enemy? Simply and solely *by the word of God.* The only weapon he employed was "*the sword of the Spirit.*" Eph. vi. 17. Though Christ was tempted, first to distrust God, then to act presumptuously, and then to commit idolatry, still his only defence was this: *"It is written"*—*"It is writ-*

ten;"—"Get thee behind me, Satan; *for it is written.*" See Deut. vi. 13; viii. 3; x. 20; comp. Luke iv. 1-13.

And when the devil, on seeing Christ's supreme regard for the authority of Scripture, quoted to him a part of Psalm xci. in a mutilated form, forthwith Jesus confounded him by saying: "*It is written again.*" Matt. iv. 7.

When his first great temptation was ended, "Jesus returned in the power of the Spirit into Galilee;—and he came to Nazareth, where he had been brought up: and, as his custom was, he went into the synagogue on the sabbath day, and stood up for to read. And there was delivered to him the book of the prophet Esaias." Luke iv. 14-19. Having read Isa. lxi. 1-3, he closed the book, gave it to the minister again, and sat down; and, while the eyes of all were fastened on him, he, began to say to them: "*This day is this Scripture fulfilled in your ears.* And all bare him witness, and wondered at the gracious words which proceeded out of his mouth." Verses 21, 22.

"After this there was a feast of the Jews; and Jesus went up to Jerusalem." John v. 1-9. While there he healed "the impotent man" at the pool of Bethesda on the Sabbath day. The Jews murmured; and after much controversy with them, Jesus said: "*Search the Scriptures;* for in them ye think ye have eternal life, and these are they *which testify of me.*" Verse 39. Hence

Christ embraces the whole of the Old Testament, which the Jews admitted to be the inspired word of God.

When the Pharisees temptingly asked the Saviour his views of marriage and divorce, he appealed to the Old Testament Scriptures as the basis of his doctrine on this subject. He replied: "*Have ye not read* (Gen. i. 27; ii. 24), that he which made them at the beginning, made them male and female, and said: For this cause shall a man leave father and mother, and shall cleave to his wife; and they twain shall be one flesh? What therefore God hath joined together, let not man put asunder." Matt. xix. 4–6.

Again, our Lord on the night of his betrayal quoted the language of Zechariah (xiii. 7), and applied it to himself, and to his disciples. Hence it will doubtless be admitted that Christ is a competent expositor; and his allusion to it is as follows: "All ye shall be offended because of me this night; *for it is written*, I will smite the Shepherd, and the sheep of the flock shall be scattered." Matt. xxvi. 31.

Again, we hear the Saviour exclaim on the cross. "My God, my God, why hast thou forsaken me?" Matt. xxvii. 46. This was the prophetical language of David, uttered more than a thousand years before its complete fulfillment. See Ps. xxii. 1. There remained still another prophecy to be fulfilled before the Saviour's death. Vinegar must be given him to drink, as the Holy Ghost had declared by the mouth of David in Psalm lxix. Accordingly, it is written: "Jesus knowing that all things were now accomplished, *that the Scripture might be fulfilled*, saith, I thirst. And they filled a sponge with vinegar, and put it upon hyssop, and put it to his mouth. When Jesus therefore had received the vinegar, he said: *It is finished;* and he bowed his head and gave up the ghost." John xix. 28–30.

And again, after his resurrection, we find the Saviour explaining the Scriptures and applying them to himself. As Cleopas and his friend communed and reasoned together on their way to Emmaus, "Jesus himself drew near and went with them." Luke xxiv. 15. "Then he said unto them, O fools, and slow of heart to believe all that the prophets have spoken; ought not Christ to have suffered these things, and to enter into his glory? And beginning at Moses and all the prophets, he expounded unto them in all the Scriptures the things concerning himself." Verses 25–27. "And they said one to another, Did not our heart burn within us, while he talked with us by the way, and while he opened to us the Scriptures?" Verse 32.

Afterwards Jesus "appeared unto the eleven as they sat at meat, and upbraided them with their unbelief and hardness of heart" (Mark xvi. 14), and said unto them: "These are the words which I spake unto you, while I was yet with you, that all things must be fulfilled which were written in the law of Moses, and in the prophets, and in the psalms, concerning me. Then opened he their understanding, that they might understand the Scriptures, and said unto them: *Thus it is written,* and thus it behooved Christ to suffer, and to rise from the dead the third day; and that repentance and remission of sins should be preached in his name among all nations, beginning at Jerusalem. And ye are witnesses of these things." Luke xxiv. 44–48.

Such is a fair specimen of the testimony of Jesus to the Inspiration of the Scriptures. He evidently believed in the *plenary and verbal Inspiration of all Scripture,* and claimed the same infallible truthfulness for the writings of Moses and the prophets, that he did for his own inspired teachings, which shall stand when heaven and earth pass away. Matt. v. 18; Luke xxi. 33. So far from admitting that the *language* of Scripture was left to the free choice and pious fancy of the sacred writers, he emphatically declares that *every word* was given by divine Inspiration, and hence "*cannot be broken.*" John x. 35.

3. My third direct proof of Inspiration is drawn *from the writings of the Apostles and Evangelists.*

The New Testament writers, like the Saviour, made the Old Testament Scriptures the *basis* of their teachings, and regarded the New as the fulfillment of the Old. They quote the writings of Moses and the Prophets as infallible proof of the truthfulness of their own doctrines, and as component parts of the word of God, equally authoritative and true with the teachings of Christ himself. They recognize the Old Testament as an essential element of "the faith once delivered to the saints"; and as containing in its doctrines, narratives, precepts, prophecies, and types, the germs of all the leading truths of the gospel. This applies both to the doctrines and duties of Christianity.

For example, Paul teaches that the typical meaning of Circumcision was *a change of heart.* "Neither," says he, "is that circumcision which is outward in the flesh:"—but "circumcision is that of the heart, in the spirit."—Rom. ii. 28, 29. Again, the apostle, in his discussion of justification by faith, illustrates the doctrine by the case of Abraham, and adds: "It was not written for his sake alone, that it (his faith) was imputed to him; but *for us also,* to whom it shall be imputed if we believe on him." Rom. iv. 22–24. And when addressing the church at Corinth on the subject of ministerial support, the apostle asks: "Say I these things as a man? or saith not the law the same also? For it is written in the law of Moses (Deut. xxv. 4): Thou shalt not muzzle the mouth of the ox that treadeth out the corn"; adding in explanation, "*For our sakes no doubt this is written.*"—"Even so hath the Lord ordained that they who preach the gospel should live of the gospel." 1 Cor. ix. 7–14. Again, Paul reminds the Corinthians of the fact, that he had declared unto them first of all, how that Christ died, was buried, and rose again the third day, "*according to the Scriptures.*" 1 Cor. xv. 1–4. And in his defence before King Agrippa, the apostle adds: "Having therefore obtained help of God, I continue unto this day, witnessing both to small and great, saying none other things than *those which the prophets and Moses did say* should come: *that Christ should suffer.*" Acts xxvi. 22, 23.

Thus Peter, also, demonstrated to the Jews from the Old Testament, that God had made that same Jesus, whom they had crucified, both Lord and Christ. Acts ii. 36. So all the apostles and evangelists taught. They not only quote distinct proof texts, but incorporate the very language of the Old Testament with their own doctrines, and thus represent the prophets in the same light as themselves. And in no way do they more clearly evince their belief in the Inspiration of the Old Testament Scriptures than by giving *collective quotations* from various books of the Bible, in order to prove some Christian doctrine. The Epistle to the Hebrews furnishes several instances of this; but the most striking example is found in Rom. iii. 10–18, where five different texts from the Psalms are combined in the same quotation with a passage from Isaiah, to prove the doctrine of human depravity and universal wickedness—the whole series commencing with the formula: "*As it is written;*" from which it necessarily results that each portion of

D

Scripture must be regarded as part of one divine whole.

Thus the New Testament writers, guided by Inspiration, combined their faith and hopes, their words and acts, with the very substance and language of the Old Testament Scriptures. Accordingly, they insist not only upon the preparatory relation of the Old Testament to the New, but also upon the permanent authority of the Old, as an *integral part* of the word of God, "which liveth and abideth forever." "For whatsoever things were written aforetime," says Paul, "were written for our learning, that we through patience and comfort of the Scriptures might have hope." Rom. xv. 4. And John, in his Apocalyptic vision, informs us, that both the Old and the New Testaments furnish the language of adoration and praise to the redeemed in heaven, who "sing the song of Moses the servant of God, and the song of the Lamb." Rev. xv. 3. So intimate, indeed, is the connection subsisting between the Old and the New Testaments, in language, thought, and design, that we are bound to regard their several parts as but different members of one organized whole; each fulfilling its own proper function, and all pointing to the Lamb of God who taketh away the sin of the world.

The New Testament writers sometimes quote literally from the Septuagint Version where it differs from the Hebrew. Thus our Lord himself sanctioned this translation in regard to marriage by quoting the words "and they twain," which are not expressed in the Hebrew (Matt. xix. 5); and Paul does the same in Eph. v. 31. In all such cases the Greek translation is followed as expressing the true sense of the original Hebrew: the idea veiled in the words of the Old Testament being thus more fully brought out in the New Testament by the same divine authority that revealed and inspired both Testaments.

On the other hand, when the Septuagint does not express the true idea of the prophets, the New Testament writers guided by Inspiration abandon it, and give their own translation of the original Hebrew. For instance, John quotes Zech. xii. 10: "They shall look on him whom they pierced" (John xix. 37), and corrects the Greek translation. Thus the Old Testament Scriptures are explained and perfected in the New Testament.

The apostles and evangelists not only quote the writings of Moses and the prophets as inspired authority, but also claim equal authority and inspiration for their own writings. They claim divine authority and plenary and verbal inspiration for all their teachings and writings, and never for a moment admit the possibility of their statements being erroneous. They enforce the obligation to receive their doctrines and obey their commands on the ground that they had been accompanied with such miracles as attest their divine authority and inspiration. See Rom. xv. 19; 2 Cor. xii. 12; Heb. ii. 4, etc. This authority they claim to be equal to that of the prophets and of Christ himself. To the Ephesian Christians Paul said: "Ye are built upon the foundation of the apostles and prophets, Jesus Christ himself being the chief corner-stone." Eph. ii. 20. Here the apostles are placed first in order, although last in point of time. And Peter exhorted his brethren to be "mindful of the words which were spoken before by the holy prophets, and of the commandment of us the apostles of the Lord and Saviour" (2 Peter iii. 2), who "have preached the gospel unto you with the Holy Ghost sent down from heaven." 1 Peter i. 12. Thus the New Testament writers claim for themselves the same divine guidance which they ascribe to those "holy men of God," who "spake as they were moved by the Holy Ghost." 2 Peter i. 21.

They not only claim plenary and verbal Inspiration and absolute truthfulness for their oral teachings, but also for their *canonical writings*. That the New Testament, like the Old, was intended as a *"memorial"* for after times, is evident from what John says of the design of his Gospel: "These *are written*, that ye might believe that Jesus is the Christ, the Son of God; and that believing, ye might have life through his name." John xx. 31. The various parts of the New Testament were successively committed to writing at the divine command and by the Inspiration of the Holy Spirit, as the existing wants of churches and individuals required it. For instance, "Jesus Christ, the faithful Witness," in his "revelation" to John, said: "What thou seest, *write in a book*, and send it unto the seven churches which are in Asia" (Rev. i. 1–11); and yet each of these epistles is styled, "*what the Spirit saith unto the churches.*" Rev. ii. 1–7. The general command to the apostle was: "Write the things which thou hast seen, and the things which are, and the things which shall be hereafter." Rev. i. 19. And the same apostle, on *twelve* different occasions, received a command to write a narrative of his visions. See, for example, Rev. ii. 12, 18; iii. 1, 7, 14; xiv. 13; xix. 9; xxi. 5. Accordingly, said Paul to the Corinthians: "If any man think himself to be a prophet, or spiritual, let him acknowledge that *the things that I have written* unto you are the commandments of the Lord." 1 Cor. xiv. 37. And to the Thessalonians the apostle said: "Stand fast, and hold the traditions (or doctrines) which ye have been taught, whether by word, *or our epistle.*" 2 Thess. ii. 15.

Nor are we to imagine that the inspiration of the apostles and evangelists extended merely to the doctrines and facts recorded: it extends alike to the *language* which they employed. Including the teachings of himself and his inspired colleagues, Paul says: " Which things we speak, not *in the words* which man's wisdom teacheth, but which *the Holy Ghost teacheth.*" 1 Cor. ii. 13. "For this cause also thank we God without ceasing," adds the apostle to the Thessalonians, "because, when ye received the word of God which ye heard of us, ye received it not as the word of men, but as it is in truth, *the word of God.*" 1 Thess. ii. 13. Now the phrase, *word of God*, necessarily implies that the Scriptures are God's, in *language* as well as matter, in *style* as well as sentiment. The divine character of Scripture language is further evident from Gal. iii. 16, where Paul says: "To Abraham and his seed were the promises made. He saith not, and to *seeds*, as of many; but as of *one*, And to thy seed, which is Christ." Here the apostle confines himself to the exposition of *a single word*, and founds his argument on the force of that one word. Now believers "are all *one* in Christ Jesus"; and if they be Christ's, then are they "Abraham's seed, and heirs according to the promise." Gal. iii. 28, 29. Hence we see that the *very words* of Scripture, equally with its doctrines and truths, are inspired; and, therefore, the Bible is the word of God, in language, manner, and thought.

From all these facts we learn the *principle* which guided the New Testament writers in the use which they have made of the Old Testament. The ancient prophets often did not fully comprehend the meaning of the pre-

BIBLE INSPIRATION. 55

dictions to which they gave utterance. The Holy Spirit, by whose inspiration they spoke and wrote, had infused a deeper significance into their words than they were able to perceive. This fact Daniel and others expressly declare. And Peter tells us, that "the prophets have inquired and searched diligently, who prophesied of the grace that should come unto you; searching what, or what manner of time the Spirit of Christ which was in them did signify, when it testified beforehand the sufferings of Christ, and the glory that should follow. Unto whom it was revealed, that not unto themselves, but unto us they did minister the things which are now reported unto you by them that have preached the gospel unto you with the Holy Ghost sent down from heaven; which things the angels desire to look into." 1 Peter i. 10-12. Both angels and prophets were diligent students of ancient prophecy. But it remained for Christ and his apostles, in the fullness of time, to comprehend the depths of prophecy and to unfold its hidden mysteries. Says Paul: "God hath revealed them unto us *by his Spirit;* for the Spirit searcheth all things, yea, the deep things of God. . . . For who hath known the mind of the Lord, that he may instruct him? But we have the mind of Christ."

1 Cor. ii. 10-16.

Our Lord, on four different occasions, promised *plenary and verbal Inspiration* to his chosen disciples (Matt x. 19, 20; Mark xiii. 11; Luke xii. 11, 12; John xiv. 16, 17,

26); and, on his departure, he repeated the promise and bid them "tarry in the city of Jerusalem," until they received the blessing. Luke xxiv. 49. The three first passages express substantially the same idea, and may be considered together:—"When they deliver you up, take no thought *how* or *what* ye shall speak; for *it shall be given you* in that same hour what ye shall speak; for it is not ye that speak, but *the Spirit of your Father* which speaketh in you." Matt. x. 19, 20; comp. Mark xiii. 11; Luke xii. 11, 12. These three promises embrace all the public occasions on which the apostles could be called upon to defend themselves, whether before councils or kings, governors or synagogues. On every such occasion the assurance was the same:—"Take no thought beforehand what ye shall speak, neither do ye premeditate; but whatsoever *shall be given you in that hour*, that speak ye: for it is not ye that speak, but *the Holy Ghost.*" Mark xiii. 11. Plenary and verbal Inspiration could not be more clearly and fully expressed than it is in these promises.

In accordance with his last great promise—"And lo! I am with you alway, even unto the end of the world" (Matt. xxviii. 20), the Saviour here gives his disciples a threefold pledge, "that in every exercise of their apostolic office, both the *form* and the *substance*, the *language* and the *thought* of their statements *should be given them* "in that same hour." (Lee, "Nature and Proofs of Inspiration," p. 247.) The apostles themselves so understood these words of our Lord; and hence Paul besought his Ephesian brethren to pray on his behalf, "that utterance may be *given* to me, that I may open my mouth boldly, to make known the mystery of the gospel." Eph. vi. 19. As before shown, the gift of Inspiration was not conferred except on special occasions, and for special purposes, and that in answer to prayer, as was the power of working miracles. And can we reasonably imagine that the apostles were thus infallibly guided when *speaking* the truth, but were left to their own fallible judgment when *recording* the same truth for the instruction of all succeeding generations? The supposition is as unreasonable as it is unscriptural.

As to the *fulfillment* of these promises, the New Testament itself enables us to form a correct opinion. When the extraordinary gift of the Holy Spirit was bestowed upon the disciples on the day of Pentecost, there was a perfect *transformation* of their whole nature, similar to that described in the words of Samuel to Saul:— "The Spirit of the Lord will come upon thee, and thou shalt be turned into another man." 1 Sam. x. 6. " And they were all filled with the Holy Ghost, and began to speak with other tongues, *as the Spirit gave them utterance.*" Acts ii. 4. " We find these poor fishermen of Galilee, whose whole tone of thought and line of conduct before their Lord's departure had remained so true to the character of 'unlearned and ignorant men,' *changed on a sudden,* into the courageous rivals of the philosophers and rhetoricians of their age. We see them, at first restless from doubts and fettered by prejudice, now immovable in their convictions and alive to each new aspect of the truth. Formerly timid and wavering, they are now fearless and resolved. Their delusive dream of temporal deliverance becomes a real assurance of eternal redemption. Their narrow estimate of the divine covenant with their nation expands under the guidance of the Holy Spirit, into the sublime conception of 'the Israel of God.'" (Lee, "Nature and Proofs of Inspiration," p. 249.)

This fact is reluctantly conceded by Dr. Paulus, a leading modern Rationalist, as quoted by Dr. Tholuck in the following words: "If we embrace in historic glance the record of the origin of Christianity, from the last evening of the life of Jesus, to the close of the fifty days next following, it is undeniable that, in that short interval, something of a nature encouraging *beyond what was ordinary* must have taken place, to transform the trembling and irresolute apostles of that evening into men exalted above all fear of death, who could exclaim before the most embittered judges of the murdered Jesus: ' *We must obey God rather than man.*'" And Tholuck adds, "that even Strauss admits this transformation in the character and conduct of the apostles to be *inexplicable*, unless something *extraordinary* be supposed to have occurred during this interval." These admissions of the opposers of plenary and verbal Inspiration are as just as they are confirmatory of the doctrine which we advocate.

Again, the promises of our Lord recorded by John, are even more comprehensive and specific. Here, as in the other pages, the extraordinary gift of the Holy Spirit is the great blessing promised:—"I will pray the Father, and he shall give you another Comforter, that he may abide with you forever,—*even the Spirit of truth* (John xiv. 16, 17); adding to relieve the misguided sorrow of his disciples: "It is expedient for you that I go away; for if I go not away, the Comforter will not come unto you." John xvi. 7. In the language of another: "The apostles who had followed their Divine Teacher during his sojourn on earth were, no doubt, acquainted with the facts of his life: but there was, as yet, no *object* of Christian Faith, in the true sense of the term, until the Lord had been received up into glory, and had triumphed over death and the grave. When he was removed from them, and his words no longer served as their guide, it became indispensable that his presence should be supplied. The suggestions of the Holy Ghost were then required in order to qualify them for their future labors:—to develop the full signification of the great events of which they had been spectators, and which now lay before them as matters of history; to give them a just insight into the divine counsels; to enable them to insert in their teaching, without interweaving any heterogeneous element, each particular circumstance as it contributed to the elucidation of the general scheme; to remind them of what had passed, without any distortion of the whole series of facts; and, in fine, *to disclose the future,* so that they might be able to decide, without error, in all the exigencies which should befall the Church."

And this, indeed, is what the Saviour promised his disciples. The Holy Spirit, who was thenceforward to supply his personal presence, is expressly styled, " *the Spirit of truth.*" "Who," says Jesus, "shall teach you all things, and bring all things to your remembrance, whatsoever I have said unto you." John xiv. 26. The Holy Spirit was not only to bring all things to their "*remembrance,*" whatsoever Christ had said unto them, but also to "*teach*" them all other needful truths, as they might be able to understand them. They had been faithfully instructed for more than three years by the Great Teacher himself, while "he spake unto them, being yet present with them"; but they still needed additional knowledge from the treasures of divine truth to fit them for their official work. Hence Jesus said: "When the Comforter is come, whom I will send unto you from the Father, even the Spirit of truth which proceedeth from the Father, he shall testify of me; and ye also shall bear witness, *because* ye have been with me from the beginning." John

BIBLE INSPIRATION. 65

communicated to him by Christ himself: "For I have received of the Lord that which I also delivered unto you." 1 Cor. xi. 23–26. Now the apostle repeatedly affirms that all his knowledge of the gospel had been thus revealed to him by Jesus Christ through the agency of the Holy Spirit; and he claims that the same was true of his fellow apostles. 1 Cor. ii. 10–16.

Moreover, the apostles and evangelists often quote and refer to each other's writings as inspired authority. Frequent instances of this occur in the Gospels, and also in the Epistles. For example, Peter expressly mentions the *"Epistles"* of Paul as of equal authority with *"the other Scriptures"* (2 Peter iii. 15, 16): "even as our beloved brother Paul also, according to the wisdom given unto him, *hath written* unto you." The New Testament writers, like those of the Old Testament, made free use of all previous Scriptures. Thus they bear united testimony to the fact, that *"All Scripture is given by inspiration of God,* and is profitable for doctrine, for reproof, for correction, for instruction in righteousness; that the man of God may be perfect, thoroughly furnished unto all good works." 2 Tim. iii. 16, 17.

Such are some of the *Direct Proofs* of Inspiration; drawn, 1. From the Writings of Moses and the Prophets; 2. From the Teachings of the Saviour; and 3. From the Writings of the Apostles and Evangelists.

E

xv. 26, 27. Here it is manifestly implied that the Holy Spirit should both testify of Christ, and impart additional knowledge to his disciples; a fact which is fully established by the following statement of the Saviour: "I have yet many things to say unto you, but ye cannot bear them now; howbeit, when he, the Spirit of truth, is come, he will guide you into all truth; and he will show you things to come. He shall glorify me; for he shall receive of mine, and shall show it unto you." John xvi. 12–14. In these words our Lord clearly teaches that the extraordinary gift of the Holy Spirit was designed to supply the need which the apostles had of further instruction in divine things, as well as to recall to their recollection "all things" which he himself had taught them. The Inspiration of the Holy Spirit was to be exerted, not only in reproducing with infallible accuracy what Christ had said to them, and in guarding them from all error in narrating and recording the acts of his life, but also in conveying to them a knowledge of "*the many things*" which Jesus had still to reveal to them, but which they could not then "*bear.*" And the additional knowledge thus to be conveyed to the disciples through the agency of the Holy Spirit was to bear the same stamp of infallibility as that already communicated to them by the Saviour in person. As before observed, our Lord here distinguishes between *Revelation* and *Inspiration;* claiming the former as his own peculiar prerogative, while he ascribes the latter to the agency of the Holy Spirit: "*He shall glorify me;* for he shall receive of *mine*, and shall *show* it unto you."

Now the promises here recorded by John, like those recorded by Matthew, Mark, and Luke, received a literal fulfillment. To this fact the apostles and evangelists bear abundant testimony in their writings. Take, for example, Peter, to whom it was given to open fully the door of faith to both Jews and Gentiles. In his first sermon after the extraordinary outpouring of the Holy Spirit on the day of Pentecost, he said to the inquiring multitude: "The promise is unto you, and to your children, *and* to all that are afar off, even as many as the Lord our God shall call." Acts ii. 39. Here the inspired apostle, in opposition to his former prejudices,—which it required a miracle to remove, Acts x. 9–29,—declares that the promise of salvation extended to the *Gentiles*, as well as to the Jews. And when "the apostles and brethren" at Jerusalem "contended with him" for going in and preaching the gospel to the Gentiles at the house of Cornelius, "Peter rehearsed the matter from the beginning, and expounded it by order unto them"—adding: "And as I began to speak, the Holy Ghost fell on them, as on us at the beginning. Then *remembered* I the word of the Lord, how that he said, John indeed baptized with water, but ye shall be baptized with the Holy Ghost." Acts xi. 1–16.

From these facts we learn *how* the twofold promise was fulfilled, that the "Holy Ghost" should "*teach*" the apostles "all things," and bring "all things" to their "*remembrance*" whatsoever Christ had said unto them. Accordingly, John, having repeated the question of the Jews, "What sign showest thou unto us?" and our Lord's reply, "Destroy this temple, and in three days I will raise it up,"—goes on to explain, "But he spoke of the temple of his body. When, therefore, he was risen from the dead, his disciples *remembered* that he had said this unto them; and they believed the Scripture, and the word which Jesus had said." John ii. 18-22. Again, the same evangelist says: "These things understood not his disciples at the first; but when Jesus was glorified, *then remembered* they that these things were written of him, and that they had done these things unto him." John xii. 16. Thus the Holy Spirit gradually *guided* the apostles and evangelists into "*all truth,*" and *recalled* to their memory "*whatsoever*" Jesus had taught them, enabling them to understand and apply the doctrines and facts of Scripture correctly, as occasion required.

Additional light is shed upon this subject by the example and teachings of Paul. For instance, in his Epistle to the Galatians, the apostle emphatically declares that the gospel which he preached was not of human origin. "For," says he, "I neither received it of man, neither was I taught it; *but by the revelation of Jesus Christ.*" Gal. i. 11, 12. This was specifically promised him by the Saviour when he was called and commissioned as the apostle to the Gentiles. Acts xxvi. 16. Hence Paul repeatedly disclaims having received his knowledge of the gospel from the other apostles, and adds:—" When it pleased God—to reveal his Son in me, that I should preach him among the heathen, immediately I conferred not with flesh and blood: neither went I up to Jerusalem to them who were apostles before me; but I went into Arabia, and returned again unto Damascus. Then after three years I went up to Jerusalem to see Peter, and abode with him fifteen days. But other of the apostles saw I none, save James the Lord's brother." Gal. i. 15–19. " Then fourteen years after, I went up again to Jerusalem. And I went up by revelation, and communicated unto them that gospel which I preached among the Gentiles. And when James, Cephas, and John, who seemed to be pillars, perceived the grace that was given unto me, they gave to me and Barnabas the right hand of fellowship, that we should go unto the heathen, and they unto the circumcision." Gal. ii. 1–9.

Of the *historical* facts of the gospel made known to Paul by direct revelation, and which enabled him to dispense with the ordinary sources of information, we need only mention the institution of the Lord's Supper; the knowledge of which he expressly tells us had been

III. THE MOST PLAUSIBLE OBJECTIONS TO INSPIRATION.

I. *It is objected that much of the Bible consists of familiar narratives, which needed no inspiration.*

It is true that both the Old and the New Testaments have a historical basis, and many of the facts and incidents recorded were known to the sacred writers. It is also true that God made use of their faculties and knowledge in the composition of the Bible. But Inspiration was none the less necessary in recording the historical parts, than in recording pure revelations. Much of the Bible was not written until long after the events occurred, and Inspiration was indispensably necessary. Without divine direction and control, Moses could never have given a correct account of creation, and of the fall of man, the promise of a Saviour, etc. Nor could the evangelists have written the life of Christ as we have it, without the Inspiration of the Holy Spirit. We have only a *synopsis* of the doings and sayings of Jesus, and no being but God could have directed the sacred writers what to record and what not to record. No uninspired men ever lived, who could have compiled the Four Gospels as we now have them. The great object of the Gospel record was the salvation of lost men, and out of all that Jesus said and did, just enough was recorded to serve that object. John xx. 30, 31. But God alone knew what was necessary to serve this important

BIBLE INSPIRATION. 67

end. Hence Jesus promised the Holy Spirit to his disciples—to guide them in their great work. John xiv. 26; xvi. 13–15. The Spirit guided them in the choice of the *words*, as well as in the selection of the facts to be recorded; so that the *entire Bible*, including its narratives, truths, and words, was written by the Inspiration of the Holy Spirit.

OBJECTIONS ANSWERED.

II. *It is objected that the evangelists contradict each other in the Gospels.*

We admit that there are some statements in their narratives which may, at first sight, appear to be at variance. But on careful examination, we find that they are not contradictory. For instance, take Matt. xx. 30; compared with Mark x. 46, and Luke xviii. 35. Matthew mentions *two* blind men, while Mark and Luke mention but *one*, without saying that there was no more than one. There is no contradiction, therefore, in the statements. Matthew is simply more full and specific in his statement. It is analogous to three witnesses in court—one is more circumstantial and full than the others; but there is no discrepancy between them.

Again, take Matt. xxvii. 5; compared with Acts i. 18. Matthew says that Judas "*went and hanged himself*," while Luke adds, that "*falling headlong he burst asunder.*" Both statements were true. He first hanged himself, and then fell as Luke informs us. There is perfect harmony in the statements.

Again, take Luke xxiv. 4; compared with Mark xvi. 5. Luke mentions *two* men or angels at the sepulchre, but Mark mentions only the *one* that rolled away the stone and addressed the women. There is no discrepancy in the statements. Mark does not say there was only one, while Luke is more specific and mentions two.

And, again, take Mark xv. 25; compared with John xix. 14. Mark says it was "*the third hour*," or nine o'clock in the morning, when they crucified Jesus; but John says it was "*about the sixth hour*," or near twelve o'clock at noon. John is indefinite, and says it was *about* the sixth hour. The whole proceedings occupied several hours, and the two evangelists may refer to different stages of the transaction. Perhaps, the true explanation of this apparent discrepancy is, that Mark adheres to the Jewish custom of reckoning the day from sunrise, while John gives the Roman method of reckoning from midnight, as we do. Even Strauss admits that this explanation is "possible."

Now, the above are the principal passages in the Gospels that even seem to conflict, and they are all susceptible of a fair and satisfactory interpretation. We have but a *synopsis* of the many things that Jesus said and did, and hence are ignorant of many of the accompanying circumstances and facts. But if we admit the truth of the Bible, we are bound to admit the *testimony* of the evangelists, though we might not be able to harmonize all their apparent discrepancies, none of which involve anything essential to salvation. Doubtless if we were in possession of all the facts in each case, we should have no difficulty in reconciling their statements. But all the ingenuity of learned infidels has not been able to show that the sacred historians have made a single mistake, nor that they contradict each other in their statements, here or elsewhere. See "*Origin and Inspiration of the Bible,*" *by Gaussen,* pp. 207, etc.

III. *It is objected that Paul disclaims inspiration in some parts of his writings.*

This objection is based upon 1 Cor. i. 16; vii. 10-12, 25, 40. In chapter i., Paul says he baptized certain persons at Corinth, and adds: "Besides, I know not whether I baptized any other;" and because he did not remember, are we not to believe what he says? He was inspired alike to tell us what he did remember and what he did not remember. Inspiration did not make him omniscient, but it insured the correctness of his statements. Jesus Christ, *as man,* knows not the day of judgment (Mark xiii. 32), though he possessed the Holy Spirit without measure. John iii. 34. This fact was recorded by Inspiration, and is therefore true.

In chapter vii., Paul says, "Unto the married I command, yet not I, but the Lord;" "but to the rest speak

I, not the Lord." The phrase, "*not I, but the Lord,*" means, that not Paul only, but the Lord Jesus also had given instructions to married persons on the subject involved. "*But to the rest speak I, not the Lord,*" i. e., Christ had not given specific directions to others in regard to marrying under peculiar circumstances, and hence Paul, under the guidance of the Holy Spirit, proceeded to instruct them; nor was he mistaken in thinking that he was actuated and controlled by "*the Spirit of God.*" Verse 40.

"*Now concerning virgins,*" etc. Verse 25. That is, the Lord Jesus Christ had given no express command concerning the marriage of virgins in times of great trials, and Paul, therefore, as an inspired apostle, advised them what to do, without giving a positive command.

So far from disclaiming inspiration for any part of his writings, Paul expressly declares, "*that the things that I write unto you are the commandments of the Lord.*" 1 Cor. xiv. 37.

IV. *It is objected that the Bible contradicts Profane History.*

What if this were true? Which should yield, the word of God, or uncertain history? But this is a mere *assumption;* we deny that the Bible anywhere contradicts trustworthy history. The apparent discrepancies relate not to facts, but merely to *Chronology* and *numbers,* which are confessedly uncertain.

On this point, however, there is great want of fairness. In ordinary writings, when authors disagree, men compare the evidence, and decide in favor of the one that has the preponderance. But not so in regard to the Bible and profane history. If any statement of Scripture seems to be at variance with that of an ordinary historian, it is taken for granted, without impartial and thorough examination, that the sacred narrative is false. Every presumption in favor of an uninspired writer is accepted without hesitation; while every statement of an apostle or prophet is subjected to the most rigid and unscrupulous criticism.

And of all books, the Bible is most exposed to such unfairness. It does not claim to be a connected history, nor to give things in chronological order. In fact, it scrupulously avoids touching on topics of common history, except where the sacred narratives absolutely require it. There are, however, some unavoidable points of contact, and skeptics have eagerly fastened on these disconnected allusions.

For instance, Luke ii. 2, incidentally connects the birth of our Saviour with the first decree of Cæsar Augustus to enroll all his provinces for taxation, and says that it occurred " when Cyrenius was governor of Syria." Strauss, and others, have boldly denied that Cyrenius was governor of Syria until some twelve years after the birth of Christ, and on the ground of this supposed mistake, they have denounced the credibility and inspiration of Luke's Gospel. But in the providence of God, facts have recently come to light, proving that Cyrenius was governor of Syria twice, first at the birth of our Lord, and then again at a later period; thus confirming the truth of the sacred narrative.

The same may be said of Paul's shipwreck on his voyage to Rome, recorded in Acts xxvii., which was denounced as irreconcilable with the geography of the Mediterranean. But a late English writer has thoroughly investigated the subject, and shown the wonderful accuracy of Luke's nautical statements, so that to-day his supposed mistakes stand as monuments of the truthfulness of the Acts of the Apostles.

And we may here add, that the historical accuracy of the Bible is strengthening every year. Discoveries in Assyria and Babylon have of late cleared up many old difficulties, and doubtless all other difficulties will ere long be removed. Wonderful progress has already been made in this direction.

V. *It is objected that the Bible is at variance with physical science.*

Now, the Bible does not pretend to teach science, nor does it address men in the language of science. It is not among the *progressive* sciences, though it is in *advance* of all science; for it was *perfect* from the lips of its Divine Author. Hence the Bible has nothing to fear from the profoundest discoveries of science. The Author of nature is the Author of the Bible, and therefore the real facts of physical science can never conflict with the Sacred Scriptures, rightly interpreted. In the language of Lord Bacon, we say: "No one Truth can be contradictory to any other Truth;" for Truth is the representation of things *as they really are*, and hence must be consistent with itself.

When properly viewed, therefore, there is not, and never can be, any conflict between true science and the word of God. They are component parts of one grand whole, and their teachings must of necessity harmonize, whether men can see it or not. Christian ministers, therefore, should hail with delight every new discovery in physical science, as a contribution to theological science. The most distinguished scientists of Europe and America, though too often silent on the subject, are not the men who array science against Christianity. It is only the skeptical votaries of science, such as Dr. Draper, Huxley, Tyndall, and others, who undertake to disparage the Sacred Scriptures; men who exalt reason above revelation, and would gladly rob the Bible of every thing *supernatural*, and degrade it to a level with their own idle speculations.

Hence they assert that the discoveries in geology disprove the Mosaic account of creation. See Gen., chapters i, ii. The Book of Genesis is a mere *compend* of creation, and is addressed to our religious faith, and not to scientific curiosity. It assigns no date for the epoch of creation. It simply says—"*In the beginning,*" referring to the *commencement* of all creation; and then traces the successive steps by which our heaven and earth arose out of chaos, in six *days,* or *periods,* of indefinite duration. The word *day* is often used in the Bible to denote an indefinite period of time. See Deut. ix. 1; Psalms xxxvii. 13; cxxxvii. 7; Rom. xiii. 12; Heb. iii. 15. Moses first states that all things were created *at a definite time,* without fixing the date; that all was created by *the Almighty fiat of Jehovah,* and not by chance or self-generation; and then proceeds to give the *order* in which our part of creation was fitted up for the residence of man, in six successive days, or periods, beginning with inorganic matter and advancing from the lowest organisms to the highest, without so much as hinting at the duration of the six preparatory days, or periods. And science clearly teaches that our globe has passed through successive stages from chaos to its present state.

Now the history of creation is *phenomenal,* and represents things as they appear to human view, and not in scientific language. The ablest exposition we have of this "phenomenal" view, was given by Hugh Miller, in his "Testimony of the Rocks." And we may safely say that modern discoveries in science are in no way opposed to the Mosaic account of creation.

Again, these votaries of science tells us, that Joshua x. 12-14 contradicts modern science, and therefore cannot be true. Bear in mind the fact, that inspiration is not responsible for the truth or falsity of what is recorded, but merely for the *correctness of the record itself.* But this occurrence was clearly *miraculous*, and hence cannot be explained on the known principles of physical science. Joshua commanded the sun and moon to stand still, and to human view they obeyed him. We know from science that it was the *earth* that stood still, and not the sun and moon. It is a matter of no consequence whether Joshua understood this fact or not. The language is *phenomenal*, and represents the event merely as it *appeared*. So our Lord and all the sacred writers speak of the sun and moon as rising and setting, and so Newton and all true philosophers represent the sun and moon as they appear to human vision. The real opposition of these skeptical scientists is to the *supernatural character* of the events, and not to its apparent conflict with science. The real point in controversy, therefore, is the *credibility* of miracles, and not the inspiration of the Scriptures.

Now, it has been clearly shown that the Bible, fairly interpreted, harmonizes with all the *established facts* of Astronomy, Ethnology, Geology, Metaphysics, and other sciences. But we must carefully distinguish between the known and settled facts of physical science, and the *speculations* of scientific men. Bible interpreters have often conceded too much to mere scientific speculations. There is not, and never can be, any conflict between the matured and real results of science and God's word, fairly interpreted.

Yet infidel scientists tell us, that the Bible cannot be true, unless it can be harmonized with science. But we ask, What science? Ancient or modern? Science of a hundred years ago? Much of that all scientists now discard. Science of to-day? No doubt much that is now called science will be repudiated a hundred years hence. The fact is, no little of the so-called science of the day is not real science; but merely the *speculations* of scientific men, which they themselves doubt. And it will be time enough to arraign God's word at the bar of science, when scientists themselves shall arrive at certain and unquestionable results. Thus far there is perfect harmony between the real meaning of Scripture and the real results of genuine and matured science; and, doubtless this will continue to be true to the end of time.

But as the God of the Bible is the God of nature, we should study his character and will, both in his word and works. Though the Bible is perfect and not among the progressive sciences, still our *knowledge* of its unfathomable truths may and should be *progressive;* and no doubt coming generations, with increased facilities, will understand many things in the Scriptures far better than we possibly can at present. And probably a more perfect knowledge of history and providence and science will contribute to that result. But certain it is that there is not now, and never can be, any real conflict between the Bible and true science.

VI. *It is objected that some parts of the Bible are indecent, and hence not inspired.*

This is the old objection urged by Thomas Payne, in his "Age of Reason," which has been answered a thousand times. And it is the main objection urged to-day by other blatant infidels, who, like Payne, are ignorant of the pure teachings of the Bible. They oppose the holy book because it condemns their unholy characters and lives. There is nothing indecent or immoral in the Bible, taken in its connection and for the purpose for which it was given. *As it is written:* "All Scripture is given by inspiration of God, and is profitable for doctrine, for reproof, for correction, and for instruction in righteousness." 2 Tim. iii. 16.

But no good man or woman ever found anything indecent or immoral in the Bible. The indecency is in the *objectors*, and not in God's holy word. As it is written: "Unto the pure all things are pure; but unto them that are defiled and unbelieving is nothing pure; but even their mind and conscience are defiled." Titus i. 15. The Bible is adapted to fallen man in every condition and relation of life; and if some of its teachings were not designed for a promiscuous assembly, still they are necessary to life and godliness; just as a pure mother says many things to her children in private that she would not repeat in public. The Bible deals with human nature in all its various aspects and phases, and the very things that scoffing infidels denounce as indecent and immoral, are designed as solemn warnings against great evils, and solemn admonitions to important duties. They tend to restrain men from immorality and to make them holy.

PRACTICAL DEDUCTIONS.

Having briefly explained the *nature* of Bible Inspiration, and given some *Direct Proofs* of the doctrine, and answered the most plausible *Objections* to Inspiration, we close with a few Practical Deductions from the subject. Hence we learn:

I. *That the Inspiration of the Bible is both plenary and verbal.*

This is absolutely true of every part and parcel of the original Hebrew and Greek Scriptures, and it is approximately true of translations into other languages. Our English Version, though susceptible of improvement, is in the main correct; and so far as it is a true representation of the original Scriptures, to that extent it is divinely inspired, and no farther. Hence the inestimable value of the original text of Scripture, and the great importance of the most faithful translations into our own and all other languages. God in his providence, has entrenched his word in the original Hebrew and Greek, and being dead languages, they never can change. Hence translations into other languages may be tested by this perfect and unchangeable standard, and to the end of time this infallible rule of faith and practice will direct our steps to happiness and heaven.

The Inspiration of the Bible, therefore, is both *plenary* and *verbal*, extending alike to its thoughts and words, and hence it is *the word of God* in the full sense of the term. There are *no degrees* in inspiration; the entire Bible and every part of it is inspired in the *same sense* and to the *same extent*. And this is as true of the most trivial as it is of the most important parts, of incidental allusions as of fundamental truths, of familiar narratives as of pure revelations, of the language as of the thoughts: so that the whole record is equally inspired; all having been made by the actuating, controlling, and guiding influence of the Holy Spirit through the agency of the inspired writers. Hence the Bible is the word of God in *matter* and *manner*, *language* and *style;* as truly as "Paradise Lost" was the product of John Milton, or the "Pilgrim's Progress" the work of John Bunyan. Accordingly, Paul says: "All Scripture is given by inspiration of God" (2 Tim. iii. 16); "*which things we speak, not in the words which man's wisdom teacheth, but which the Holy Ghost teacheth.*" 1 Cor. ii. 13.

Speaking of these words of Paul, Dr. Thomas Armitage, of New York, says: "He not only attributes the substance of his revelation to the Holy Spirit, but also the *words* in which it was expressed. The things were taught in *words*, but these were not chosen by his own 'wisdom,' they were 'taught by the Spirit,' so that the form of the revelation harmonized with the substance, the words with the things, and the things with the words. The Holy Spirit presided so jealously over the things which were put into Paul's manuscript, that he selected the *words*, in order that the apostle should commit no error in transmitting the things."

Dr. Charles Hodge, in representing Paul as "clothing the truths of the Spirit in the words of the Spirit," says: "There is neither in the Bible nor in the writings of men a simpler or clearer statement of the doctrines of revelation and inspiration. Revelation is the act of communicating divine knowledge to the mind. Inspiration is the act of the same Spirit controlling those who make the truth known to others. The thoughts, the truths made known, and the *words* in which they are recorded, are declared to be equally from the Spirit. This, from first to last, has been the doctrine of the Church, notwithstanding the endless diversity of speculations in which theologians have indulged on the subject. This, then, is the ground on which the sacred writers rested their claims. They were the mere organs of God. They were his messengers. Those who heard them heard God, and those who refused to hear them refused to hear God." ("Examiner," June 17, 1880).

It is evident, therefore, that the Inspiration of the Bible is both plenary and verbal, including the *ideas*, *words*, and *form*, and it extends alike to the *entire record*, stamping the whole as "the word of God." In the language of Rev. C. H. Spurgeon, of London: "We cannot but express our sense of the superficiality of the best and most laborious of comments, when compared with the bottomless depths of the sacred word, nor can we refrain from uttering our growing conviction that the Scriptures possess a *verbal* as well as a *plenary* inspiration; indeed, we are quite unable to see how they could have the one without the other. So much of meaning dwells in the turn of an expression, the tense of a verb, or the number of a noun, that we believe in the inspiration of the *words themselves;* certainly the words are the things *written* and the only things that can be written—for the refined spirit of a passage is not the creature of pen and ink. Our Lord's favorite sentence, 'It is written,' must of necessity apply to the *words;* for only words are written."

True, the Inspiration of the writers and that of their writings were necessarily connected as cause and effect, and should never be separated. Inspired men *spoke* and *wrote* as they were *directed* and *moved* by the

Holy Spirit, and consequently what they spoke and wrote was thus given by inspiration of God, and therefore is *his word* in thought, language, and form.

Accordingly, J. M. Pendleton, D. D., says: "Now as to Inspiration in the writer and not primarily in the *writings:* How is this? A writer uses *words* in writing. How then can a writer be inspired and his words be uninspired? The inspiration he feels in his soul communicates itself to what he writes, and this is the reason why we have the Bible. But to make the matter still plainer, let us substitute *speaking* for writing. We read that 'holy men spoke as they were moved by the Holy Ghost,' or as the Anglo-American version has it, 'spoke from God, being moved by the Holy Ghost.' These men, these holy men, spoke *from God;* that is, what they said came from God. They were *moved by the Holy Spirit* to speak what they said. They could not speak without *words*, and therefore their words were inseparable from their inspiration. The distinction between the inspiration of men and the inspiration of *words* spoken or written by them is obviously untenable." (Ford's "Christian Repository," December, 1883.)

II. *The Bible, like its Incarnate Author, is both divine and human, combined in harmonious and perfect union.*

It is thoroughly divine and thoroughly human, being assimilated and combined into one homogeneous organism by the vital energy of the Holy Spirit, so as to constitute the entire Bible and every part of it *the word of God*. Every page bears unmistakable evidence of a divine and human element, so blended together as to form one harmonious whole. The Holy Spirit embraced the entire activity of the inspired writers, and so employed their faculties and knowledge and language, as to render the whole Bible the word of God, while it bears the stamp of the human agents.

Nor does the human element involve error or imperfection in the Scriptures. This might have been so, but for the actuating and controlling influence of the Holy Spirit in and over the inspired writers. The union of the divine and human elements in the Bible is analogous to the incarnation of Jesus Christ, who was as truly man as he was God, and yet one person, perfectly free from all error and sin. The Bible is holy and pure, and contains the whole truth without any mistake or error, because it was dictated by the Holy Spirit.

And the divine and human elements in Scripture must be viewed in their true relations to each other. Both elements exist in the Bible, and both were necessary in a revelation from God to man. God's plan was to speak to man *through* man, and thus adapt his word to human comprehension. In the language of Dr. A. H. Strong, President of Rochester Theological Seminary, we say:

"The exaggeration of the divine element seems to us

as serious an error as the exaggeration of the human...
When we lose sight of the real human authorship of the sacred books, we incur a loss comparable only to that which we should sustain by letting go the human side of our Redeemer's person. A great part of the power of the Bible over us, like the attraction of Christ, arises from its coming to us with the voice and the sympathies of our common humanity. Inspiration took into the account this fact. It therefore did not remove, but rather pressed into service, all the personal peculiarities of the writers, together with their defects of culture and literary style. In fact, every imperfection not inconsistent with truth in a human composition may exist in inspired Scripture. The Bible is 'the word of God,' but we may also say of it, in a peculiar sense, that it is 'the word made flesh.' It presents to us truth in human forms. It is a revelation, not for a select class, but for the common mind. And rightly understood, this very humanity of the Bible is one of the best proofs of its divinity." (In "Examiner.")

Hence it is evident that the Bible, like its Incarnate Author, is both human and divine, combined in harmonious and perfect union.

III. *The whole Bible is inspired, and therefore is the word of God.*

The Bible is one organized whole, embracing all its parts. The entire book, from Genesis to Revelation, as a unit, is God's word, each of whose parts is essential to the completeness of the whole, and all divinely inspired, and therefore a perfect revelation from God to man. Yet this truth is called in question, not only by skeptics, but by some misguided Christian ministers and writers. They admit the general truthfulness of the Bible, and say it "*contains* the word of God," while they deny the inspiration of such parts as do not suit their peculiar views. Especially is this the case with the Old Testament, and the historical parts of the New. They differ widely as to what parts are inspired and what are not, and each accepts or rejects for himself, until the whole is virtually discarded. Now, we boldly affirm that the whole Bible, and every part of it, is divinely inspired, and therefore not only " contains " the word of God, but *is itself* his word, embracing its matter, language, and form; and this is equally true of the Old and the New Testaments. Let us, then, briefly notice some of the arguments in support of this view.

(1) The *Unity* of the Bible is one strong proof of its divine origin and inspiration. In the truthful language of "The Examiner," we say: "No intelligent student of the Bible can have failed to notice its singular *unity* of spirit and purpose. Wonderful in its diversity of structure beyond all other books, it is one in its grand underlying thought. Like a great organ, it has its many stops, but under and supporting all is the mighty diapason note

of redemption for fallen man. And this is one of the strongest proofs of the inspiration of the whole Bible."

"This divine record, comprising the two great divisions of Old and New Testament, presents itself to the acceptance of mankind as one organized whole; as an elaborate structure whose various parts conspire to the attainment of one definite end, the entire edifice being constructed according to one grand design. That one end is the salvation of man—that grand design is the economy of Redemption." (Lee, "Inspiration of Scripture," p. 28. Also Westcott's "Introduction," p. 334.)

As Horne forcibly states the argument in his "Introduction to the Study of the Bible," we say: "In the Scriptures there is no dissent or contradiction. They are not a book compiled by a single author, nor by many hands acting in confederacy in the same age; for in such case there would be no difficulty in composing a consistent scheme; nor would it be astonishing to find the several parts in a just and close connection. But most of the writers of the Scriptures lived at very different times, and in distant places, through the long space of about sixteeen hundred years; so that there could be no confederacy or collusion; and yet their relations agree with and mutually support each other. . . . The holy writers, men of different education, faculties, and occupations—prophets, evangelists, apostles—notwithstanding the diversity of time and place, the variety of matter, consisting of mysteries of providence as well as mysteries of faith, yet all concur uniformly in carrying on one consistent plan of supernatural doctrines; all constantly propose the same invariable truth, flowing from the same fountain through different channels. Can you find *one* writer contradicting the statements or opinions of his predecessor? One historian who disputes any fact which another has stated? Is there in the prophets any discrepancy in doctrines, precepts, or predictions? However they vary in style, or manner, or illustration, the sentiment and the morality are the same. The same remarks apply to the New Testament. The leading doctrines of Christianity harmonize together; one writer may enlarge upon and explain what another has said, may add to his account, and carry it further; but he *never* contradicts him. . . . Whence, then, arises this harmony of Scripture? Had the writers been under no peculiar divine influence, they would have reasoned and speculated like others, and their writings would have opposed each other. But if they were inspired—if they all spoke and wrote under the same Spirit—then is this harmony accounted for: and it is impossible to account for it on any other principle."

And this unity of the Bible, in the words of Dr. Lange, "proves it to be the word of God. It exerts a power within and beyond itself; it sheds a light upon itself; it radiates its light from its mighty living centre—the world-redeeming Christ—to every part, and reflects it from each part to every other, and back upon the central truth again."

(2) The *Stamp* of Inspiration is found on every page of the Bible. Not only in its wonderful unity of spirit and purpose do we see proof of the supernatural origin of the Bible, but in its *matter, manner,* and *form,* it bears "the image and superscription" of its Divine Author. Doubtless it was this *mark* of divine Inspiration that enabled Ezra, "the scribe," to identify the several books of the Old Testament as we now have them, and to exclude the *Apocryphal* Books from the canon of revelation. And it was the same *divine stamp* that guided the servants of God about the close of the first century, in selecting the inspired books of the New Testament, and in rejecting the many Apocryphal Gospels and Epistles from the canon of Scripture. The Bible is its own witness, and stands alone among books. The sacred writings of Pagan nations, whatever may be their excellences, bear unmistakable marks of their human origin.

"The Bible alone," adds Dr. Bright, "supports its claim to be a revelation from God by its own *intrinsic character.* It deals with subjects transcending the utmost stretch of unaided human imagination, and always with a lofty simplicity and power of diction unequaled in the writings of any human author. Even the plainest historical records bear the impress of more than human intelligence. They are not continuous, but elective, and the facts narrated illustrate, not the history of a people, but 'the ways of God to men.' Frequently a single sentence covers an epoch. Personal biographies often occupy more space than the record of centuries. But through all this apparently unphilosophic arrangement, careful study shows us '*an eternal purpose.*' Men do not thus write history; those who wrote the Bible record were actuated by an influence working on them *from without*, and penned the word or preserved the record which divine wisdom intended for the instruction of mankind in all ages.

"But more than this, the Bible shows its superhuman origin in the fact, that it is *a heart-searching book*. It not only makes known to us things which we could not possibly have discovered for ourselves—such as the creation and the fall—but it reveals to us *ourselves*, and so completely satisfies the longings and necessities of our moral being that, by following its teachings, we may be consciously made better and higher in character and life. And this is as true of the Old as of the New Testament; for while the latter points out the method, the former shows us the necessity of redemption from the bondage of sin. 'For the word of God is quick and powerful, and sharper than any two-edged sword, piercing even to the dividing asunder of soul and spirit, and of the joints and marrow, and is a discerner of the thoughts and intents of the heart.' Heb. iv. 12.

"Furthermore, we have the evidence of *fulfilled prophecy* in proof of the Inspiration of the Old Testament. The entire Old Testament is itself a prophecy of the New; and teems with prophetic *fore-looking*, growing brighter and stronger as the ages passed, of the coming Saviour. None but he who sees the end from the beginning, and who orders everything after the counsel of his own will, could have so opened the secrets of the future to mortal vision. 'For the prophecy came not in old time by the will of man; but holy men of God spake as they were moved by the Holy Ghost.' 2 Peter i. 21.

"And finally, we see the *stamp* of Inspiration upon the Hebrew Scriptures in the thorough candor of its records. Its noblest characters are painted with a more than pre-Raphaelite realism. Their sins, their follies, their waywardness, as well as their noble traits, are unsparingly portrayed. There are no 'heroes' in the Bible, in the romantic sense. They are *men* 'of like passions with ourselves,' but ennobled and made great through a living faith in a living God." Heb., xi. chapter.

(3) But *the Old Testament in the New* is the crowning proof of the divine origin and Inspiration of the Bible. (See pp. 38–65.) The Saviour and his apostles everywhere speak of the Old Testament Scriptures as the oracles of God, the Holy Scriptures, the word of God, and assert their divine authorship as the inspired source of spiritual knowledge and instruction in righteousness.

That the "Scriptures" thus designated are the books of the Old Testament, as we now have them, cannot be questioned. They existed in two forms—in the Hebrew originals and in a Greek translation, from both of which Christ and his apostles frequently quoted. The Old Testament, divided into "the Law, the Prophets, and the Psalms," was the great storehouse from which the Saviour, the evangelists, and the apostles drew their instructions and proofs, to establish, illustrate, and sustain the truth and divine authority of the New Dispensation. They never doubted the divine origin and Inspiration of the Old Testament. They based their claims to be heard and obeyed upon its predictions respecting the Messiah, in whom all found their complete fulfillment. How strange, then, that any professed believer in Christ, and especially any professed minister of Jesus, should call in question these very Scriptures, upon which the Saviour himself rested the sole claims of his Messiahship!

Hence we see that the whole Bible is divinely inspired, and, therefore, is the infallible word of God.

IV. *Finally, we learn the claims of the Bible upon all, and especially upon Baptists.*

It is the inspired word of God, and therefore all should read and study it diligently, and endeavor to understand it. Those who can, should examine it in the original Hebrew and Greek; and all should study it in the most faithful versions, with the best helps they can obtain.

We are expressly commanded to "Search the Scriptures"; and to "let the word of Christ dwell in us richly." John v. 39; Col. iii. 16.

It is also our duty to study and teach the Bible in our families, Sunday-schools, and churches, and to exemplify its truths in our lives. The *Bible itself* should be used by all, and not mere expositions, leaflets, and papers. There is no substitute for the Bible; all should read and study the word of God for themselves. Small children may understand enough of the Holy Scriptures to make them wise unto salvation, through faith in Christ Jesus. 2 Tim. iii. 15. And our spiritual growth depends essentially upon the pure milk of God's word. 1 Peter ii. 1-3. It fortifies us against temptation, and preserves us from all error and sin. Ps. cxix. 9, 11; 2 Peter i. 5; iii. 18.

And of all people, the Baptists should love the Bible most, and seek to circulate it among all classes. It is our only authoritative creed, our only rule of faith and practice. The Bible, and the Bible alone, is the religion of Baptists. Our motto should be: "The word of God faithfully translated into all languages and dialects." And we should hold forth the word of life to those who are perishing for the lack of knowledge. We are under peculiar obligations to preach and send the Bible to every creature in all the world.

THE END.

www.ingramcontent.com/pod-product-compliance
Lightning Source LLC
Chambersburg PA
CBHW032250080426

42735CB00008B/1075